THE PSYCHOLOGY OF PREJUDICE

Why do we develop extreme attitudes to others? Can our personality contribute to our prejudices? How do we reduce prejudice and discrimination?

The Psychology of Prejudice explores different forms of prejudice and discrimination, from racial jokes to genocide. It looks at what might cause our prejudiced attitudes, including our personalities, social influences, group identity, and evolutionary factors, and how prejudice can be reduced through education, campaigning, and consciousness raising.

Offering insights into a topic of great public concern and debate, *The Psychology of Prejudice* shows us how we can confront our prejudiced attitudes and contribute to greater tolerance and understanding.

Richard Gross has been publishing psychology texts for more than 30 years, including undergraduate textbooks.

D0162200

THE PSYCHOLOGY OF EVERYTHING

People are fascinated by psychology, and what makes humans tick. Why do we think and behave the way we do? We've all met armchair psychologists claiming to have the answers, and people that ask if psychologists can tell what they're thinking. The Psychology of Everything is a series of books which debunk the popular myths and pseudo-science surrounding some of life's biggest questions.

The series explores the hidden psychological factors that drive us, from our subconscious desires and aversions, to our natural social instincts. Absorbing, informative, and always intriguing, each book is written by an expert in the field, examining how research-based knowledge compares with popular wisdom, and showing how psychology can truly enrich our understanding of modern life.

Applying a psychological lens to an array of topics and contemporary concerns – from sex, to fashion, to conspiracy theories – The Psychology of Everything will make you look at everything in a new way.

Titles in the series:

For further information about this series please visit
www.routledgetextbooks.com/textbooks/thepsychologyofeverything/

THE PSYCHOLOGY OF PREJUDICE

RICHARD GROSS

Routledge
Taylor & Francis Group

LONDON AND NEW YORK

First published 2021
by Routledge
2 Park Square, Milton Park, Abingdon, Oxon OX14 4RN

and by Routledge
52 Vanderbilt Avenue, New York, NY 10017

Routledge is an imprint of the Taylor & Francis Group, an informa business

British Library Cataloguing-in-Publication Data
A catalogue record for this book is available from the British Library

Library of Congress Cataloging-in-Publication Data
A catalog record for this book has been requested

ISBN: 978-0-367-53464-6 (hbk)
ISBN: 978-0-367-53463-9 (pbk)
ISBN: 978-1-003-08204-0 (ebk)

Typeset in Joanna
by Apex CoVantage, LLC

Printed and bound by CPI Group (UK) Ltd, Croydon, CR0 4YY

CONTENTS

1

WHAT DO WE MEAN BY 'PREJUDICE'?

INTRODUCTION AND PLAN OF THE BOOK

Like many – if not most – aspects of human behaviour, to fully understand the nature of prejudice we need to draw on a wide range of disciplines, including psychology, sociology, history, anthropology and biology. Even within psychology, there are a number of different, albeit complementary, approaches to understanding prejudice, and Chapters 3, 4 and 5 each focus on one of these approaches. Chapter 6 discusses attempts to reduce prejudice and discrimination.

This chapter attempts to define some of the basic terms that will recur throughout the book, including prejudice as an (extreme) attitude, different forms that discrimination can take (including dehumanization and infrahumanization) and the distinction between prejudice as an attitude and as ideology.

Chapter 2 describes how prejudice, particularly racism, arose within biology, psychology and psychiatry. The concept of 'race', which has become so controversial in recent years, was given scientific respectability by Darwin's study of human evolution, but it helped to justify the views of eugenicists, who wished to control 'breeding' within certain racial and other 'undesirable' groups. In turn, the influence of eugenics was felt in the rise of mass intelligence testing in the

U.S. in World War I; this, in turn, helped justify anti-immigration legislation as Nazism took hold in Germany. While racism and sexism are also evident within psychiatry, it was heterosexism (anti-homosexual prejudice) that has been most evident until quite recently in defining, diagnosing and treating psychological abnormality.

Chapter 3 focuses on the *personality approach*, that is, the attempt to explain prejudice as one form of individual differences based on particular personality characteristics. Most famously, the *authoritarian personality* was an attempt to explain anti-Semitism in Nazi Germany in terms of susceptibility to fascist ideology. Its critics offered alternative personality accounts, including *dogmatism* and *tough-mindedness*.

Chapter 4 begins where Chapter 3 ends, by pointing out that even if personality factors are involved, they cannot account for how particular (racial) groups become the target for hostility and discrimination at different times within the same society. The focus here is on *environmental* influences, including *social norms*, which dictate when and where prejudice and discrimination are acceptable and/or required (as in apartheid South Africa), the *media* (including the way they generate stereotypes and how the Internet can contribute to terrorism) and *competition for limited resources* (winners and losers are two sides of a coin).

Chapter 5 focuses on the last major approach, namely, *group membership*. While some have argued that competition with other groups is a sufficient cause of prejudice and discrimination, the focus on group membership turns this on its head: competition, far from being sufficient, may not even be necessary. Instead, the mere fact of belonging to a particular group (the ingroup) is sufficient to favour the ingroup and discriminate against the outgroup (to which the individual doesn't belong). Experimentally, this claim has been tested in the form of the *minimal* (arbitrary/random) *group*, which, in turn, has generated *social identity theory*: our *personal* (individual) *identity* is inextricably tied to our *social identity* (the groups we belong to).

The final chapter, **Chapter 6**, discusses attempts to reduce prejudice and discrimination. While how this could be achieved can be inferred from each of these three main approaches, only the *contact* *hypothesis* confronts this issue directly and explicitly. *Intergroup contact* can take many forms, face to face or via media, direct and indirect, short term or longer term, but the overall picture that emerges is an optimistic one. However, the nature of human thinking combined with the way society operates probably set limits on how far prejudice and discrimination reduction can go.

SOME INTRODUCTORY OBSERVATIONS: 'PREJUDICE' AND 'BIAS'

Try making some associations around the term 'prejudice': what comes to mind? Terms that denote 'isms' (e.g. racism, sexism, ageism) are likely candidates; these arguably are the most common examples that get discussed in the media and in everyday conversations. Other less common examples include heterosexism, anti-Semitism (sometimes classified as a form of racism), classism and sizeism.

What all these examples of prejudice have in common is an 'against-ness', an *anti* position towards the targeted social groups (sometimes referred to as *negative* or *hostile* prejudice):

- Until quite recently, much of the psychological theory and research into prejudice was concerned with *racism*: 'the quite specific belief that cultural differences between ethnic groups are of biological origin and that groups should be ranked in worth'.[1] This is closely related to *ethnocentrism*,[2] the strong human tendency to use our own cultural or ethnic group's norms and values to define what's 'natural' and 'correct' for everyone ('reality').[3] Implicitly, at least, one's own group is *superior* to other groups.
- *Anti-Semitism* is a specific form of racism which, in practice, focuses on Jewish people (although 'semitic' peoples actually include Arabs and other Middle Eastern populations).
- *Sexism* is similar to racism, but race/cultural or ethnic background is replaced by *gender* (that is, our social roles of man or woman). So, strictly, what's commonly called 'sexism' should be called *genderism* (since biological sex – 'male'/'female' – is distinct from gender).

So, if women's behaviour differs from men's, the former is often judged to be deficient or even abnormal in some way. As in ethnocentrism, *androcentrism* – male-centredness or the *masculinist bias* – involves taking men's behaviour – implicitly or explicitly – as the 'standard' or norm against which women's behaviour is compared.

- In *heterosexism*, heterosexuality – both female and male – is taken, implicitly or explicitly, as the norm, so that male or female homosexuality (or bi-sexuality) is taken to be abnormal.
- Similarly, *ageism* involves the perceived superiority of young(er) people, *classism* takes certain socioeconomic groups – usually those from 'privileged'/upper-middle-class backgrounds as superior, and *sizeism* involves denigration of 'fat'/overweight/obese people (by those who aren't).

What these examples show is that there are always (at least) two sides to the coin of prejudice; in the case of sexism, for example, female inferiority is the other side of the male superiority coin. Sometimes, rather than expressing the 'anti' side, it might be the 'pro' side of the coin that someone wishes to highlight. In these cases, it might be more accurate to use the term 'bias' than 'prejudice'. We usually think of bias as being *in favour of* or *pro* some group (as in the 'masculinist bias'). While these are two sides of a coin, being in favour of X seems far more acceptable – morally and socially – than being against Y.

However, according to the *Oxford Illustrated Dictionary*,[4] *bias* means 'inclination, predisposition, prejudice, influence'; similarly, the *Reader's Digest Universal Dictionary*[5] defines *bias* as 'preference or inclination that inhibits impartial judgement; prejudice'. Conversely, the former defines *prejudice* as 'an adverse judgement/opinion formed beforehand or without knowledge/examination of the facts . . . biased' and 'preconceived opinion, bias', respectively.

While these dictionary definitions suggest that 'prejudice' and 'bias' are *interchangeable*, in common usage there are important differences, and psychologists use the terms to refer to quite different things (often, different aspects of our thinking). For example, while both refer to some preconceived opinion or attitude, 'bias' conveys a leaning towards or *preference* for something (be it a particular football team, political party) – the 'pro' side of the coin – whereas 'prejudice' conveys a pre-*judgement* without knowledge or examination of the facts (e.g. the guilt of someone accused of a crime).

Strictly, both may be either 'for' or 'against', but, again, in common usage, 'bias' tends to convey a favourable, positive preference for something, while 'prejudice' tends to convey the opposite. So, while we may describe football referees as *biased* in favour of the home team (especially one of the 'big clubs'), if we claim that the person accused of a violent crime is probably guilty because they're black, then we'd be described as (racially) *prejudiced*. Instead of being impartial, the biased referee (unconsciously) awards the home team more free kicks and the prejudiced (white) person makes up their mind about the accused's guilt/innocence without first examining the evidence.

SOME EXAMPLES OF BIASED THINKING

Within psychology, 'bias' is often used to denote a tendency – usually unconscious – to think in a particular way about, for example, the causes of people's behaviour. For example, quite understandably, we don't want to admit to being incompetent, so we're more likely to attribute our failures to *external* factors, often beyond our control (such as other people's incompetence); this *self-protecting bias* helps to protect our self-esteem. However, we're quite happy to take the credit for our successes (which we trust reflect *internal/dispositional* factors, such as intelligence or skill); this *self-enhancing bias* enhances our self-esteem. Together, they constitute the *self-serving bias* (SSB).[6]

The *fundamental attribution error* (FAE)[7] refers to the general tendency to overestimate the importance of personal or dispositional factors (i.e. internal), as distinct from environmental factors (i.e. external), as causes of behaviour. As the SSB shows, when judging our own behaviour this tendency mostly applies when we've behaved in a socially positive/desirable way. But what about when we're judging someone else's behaviour?

The *ultimate attribution error* (UAE)[8] is an extension of the FAE applied to the *group* context. Social psychologists see *intergroup relations* – especially *intergroup conflict* – as crucial for understanding prejudice (see Chapter 5).

Our ingroups are both those that we actually belong to (*membership* groups), such as 'Tottenham Hotspur supporters' and 'England cricket fans', and those that we aspire to belong to (*reference* groups), such as 'Member of Parliament' and 'professional actor'. All other groups are outgroups. As well as 'intergroup conflict', psychologists talk about *ingroup bias*, a favourable perception of one's membership or reference group relative to outgroups; however, this doesn't necessarily imply a hostile or aggressive prejudice against the latter.

As far as the UAE is concerned, the nature of intergroup relations shapes the *different* attributions that group members make for the *same* behaviour depending on whose behaviour it is – a member of the ingroup or the outgroup. People are more likely to make *internal* attributions for their ingroup's positive, socially desirable behaviour and *external* attributions for the same positive behaviour displayed by the outgroup. In contrast, negative, socially undesirable behaviour would be attributed to *internal* factors if the outgroup is involved (it's part of the prejudiced view of the outgroup) but *externally* if displayed by an ingroup member (it's blamed on 'bad luck' or some unpredictable environmental circumstances). This way of explaining ingroup and outgroup behaviour is *self-serving*, since our self-esteem is determined partly by the performance of those groups.

PREJUDICE AS AN ATTITUDE AND AS IDEOLOGY

We began our attempts to define prejudice by identifying examples, suggesting that racism, sexism etc. are what we normally think of as prejudice. Psychological definitions of prejudice usually include the term 'attitude', and attitudes refer to the thinking of individuals.

Psychologists regard prejudice as an *extreme* attitude: it possesses all the characteristics of other attitudes, but in certain respects, these are exaggerated in the case of sexist or racist attitudes. So what are these characteristics that all attitudes have in common?

The *cognitive* (i.e. mental) component is the *stereotype*. Stereotypes can be thought of as a special kind of *implicit personality theory* (IPT); these are the intuitive theories we have about 'what makes people tick' and can either refer to individuals (e.g. 'redheads have fiery tempers' or 'high foreheads are a sign of superior intelligence') or – as in stereotypes – to an entire social group (e.g. 'women are . . .' or 'black people are . . .').

Stereotypes were originally defined as 'pictures in our head'.[9] For a long time, psychologists took the view that such over-generalizations were inherently bad: not only were they seen as false and illogical, but they were only held by people who were prejudiced. However, most psychologists today would accept that stereotypes are 'categories about people'.[10] Categories in general – and stereotypes in particular – are mental *shortcuts*; they're universal and inevitable, 'an intrinsic, essential and primitive aspect of cognition'.[11] They help us deal with a potentially overwhelming amount of information that constantly bombards our senses. To this extent, there's nothing unique about stereotypes; it's really only when they are combined with the other components of attitudes (especially the *affective*) that they constitute prejudice and become dangerous.

GENDER STEREOTYPES AND TELEVISION ADVERTISING

One way in which *gender stereotypes* have been investigated is in relation to television advertising. American research in the 1970s reported that TV commercials weren't responsive to changes in sex roles taking place since the late 1960s. For example, one study found that women were portrayed as housewife/mother in 56 per cent of their advertising roles, compared with 14 per cent of men (as husband/father);[12] a second study[13] reported 45 per cent and 15 per cent, respectively. A number of studies (including the first) concluded that women were overrepresented in domestic settings and underrepresented in out-of-home occupations.[14]

The first major British study[15] was an attempt to replicate the last-cited U.S. study; it reached essentially the same conclusions. Adult males and females were portrayed in markedly different ways, consistent with traditional sex/gender roles: males were typically shown as having expertise and authority, as being objective and knowledgeable about reasons for buying particular products, as occupying autonomous roles and as being concerned with the practical consequences of product purchase. By contrast, females were typically portrayed as product *consumers*, *lacking* knowledge for buying particular products, occupying *dependent* social roles and concerned with the *social* consequences of product purchase.

A later American study[16] aimed to determine whether how women were portrayed had undergone significant change since the 1972 Dominick and Rauch study. While they were portrayed in a wider range of occupations and appeared more frequently in non-domestic settings, there were no changes regarding product type, voice-over announcer, on-camera product representative and age categories.

A quite recent study[17] confirmed the finding of the early studies regarding a *culture lag* between the changing roles of women and men in domestic and occupational roles and how they have been traditionally portrayed in TV advertising. However, women are being presented more positively relative to their potential and capabilities, and men are being portrayed as 'softer' while interacting with their children and in more egalitarian roles.

While all the studies cited so far are British or American, a recent study[18] compared the stereotypical depiction of women and men from a total of 13 Asian, American and European countries. The main conclusion was that gender stereotypes regarding primary character, voice-over, home or work setting and so on, can be found around the world. The researchers concluded that stereotyping is independent of the gender equality prevalent in a particular country; hence, the role of a specific culture in shaping gender stereotypes in TV advertising is less important than commonly thought.

- The *affective* (i.e. emotional) component is (usually) a *strong feeling of hostility* or *antipathy*. The 'againstness' of prejudice is captured in this affective component, making it crucial.[19] This is illustrated by the finding that individual differences in affective/emotional prejudice are correlated with *discrimination* (which relates to the third component, i.e. the behavioural) more strongly than stereotypes are.[20] For example, affective reactions to gay men predict discrimination far better than do stereotypes.[21]

- The *behavioural* component can take various forms. Gordon Allport,[22] arguably (still) the most influential and frequently cited psychologist in relation to prejudice, identified five stages of the behavioural component, increasing in the potential harm they can produce for the victims.

  1 *Antilocution*: hostile talk, verbal denigration and insult, racist/sexist jokes
  2 *Avoidance*: keeping a distance, but without actively inflicting harm
  3 *Discrimination*: exclusion from housing, civil rights, employment etc.
  4 *Physical attack*: violence against the person and property
  5 *Extermination*: indiscriminate violence against an entire group (including genocide).

While Allport reserves 'discrimination' for exclusion from housing etc., most psychologists use the term far more broadly to cover any and all behaviours aimed at harming members of particular social, ethnic, religious etc. outgroups simply because they belong to those groups.

If we accuse someone of, say, 'being racist', it would be more accurate to accuse them of 'being racially prejudiced': what we're attributing to them is an attitude, which, as we've seen, is a feature of how *individuals* think about the world. Strictly, racism, sexism and the other 'isms' are *ideologies*, which are a feature of whole *societies*; prejudiced attitudes reflect these society-wide beliefs and feelings.[23,24]

CAN PEOPLE DISCRIMINATE WITHOUT BEING PREJUDICED?

As we noted earlier, the affective component (hostile feelings) is a more important/better predictor of anti-gay discrimination than is the cognitive component (stereotypes); also, and more generally, these hostile feelings are more strongly correlated with discrimination than are stereotypes. What this tells us is that while all three components together constitute an attitude, they're not perfectly correlated: they can be inconsistent with each other. This can mean a number of different things:

1 You may hold stereotyped beliefs about, say, lesbians but not necessarily feel particularly hostile towards them, and you wouldn't dream of insulting someone – or in any other way discriminating against her – for being lesbian.
2 You may harbour hostile feelings without necessarily knowing why; your stereotyped beliefs may not, logically or rationally, account for your hostility.
3 You may be very clear as to why you dislike certain outgroups but still not express these feelings and beliefs through discriminatory behaviour. A famous demonstration of this came in a study reported in 1934.[25] Beginning in 1930 and for the next two years, Richard LaPiere, an American sociologist, travelled around the U.S. with a young Chinese couple (a student and his wife). This was a time of widespread anti-Oriental attitudes, so LaPiere and his friends expected to encounter discrimination which would make it difficult for them to find accommodation. However, in the course of 10,000 miles of travel, they were refused entry just once, being allowed into 66 hotels, auto-camps and 'tourist homes'. They were also served in 184 restaurants and cafes and treated unusually well in 72 of them. Six months after the end of their travels, LaPiere wrote to each of the 251 establishments visited, asking, 'Will you accept members of the Chinese race as guests in your establishment?' Of the 128 that responded, 91 per cent gave an emphatic 'No', one gave an unqualified 'Yes', and the rest said 'Undecided: depends upon circumstances'.

HOW CAN WE ACCOUNT FOR THESE FINDINGS?

It's widely accepted by psychologists that attitudes represent only a *predisposition* to behave in a particular way; how we *actually* behave in any situation will depend on several factors, including the likely consequences of our actions, how we think others will evaluate us, expected ways of behaving in particular situations and so on. There may also be specific *situational factors* that influence us. For example, in the LaPiere study, the Chinese couple's expensive clothes and luggage, together with their politeness and the presence of LaPiere himself, may have made it more difficult to display cognitive and affective prejudice; manifest, overt behaviour may often represent a compromise between prejudice and socially acceptable – or tolerable – behaviour.

4 In another demonstration of the impact of environmental factors, you may act in a discriminating way without being prejudiced in the cognitive and affective senses. For example, traditionally, overt anti-black discrimination has been greater in the southern U.S. But white Southerners haven't scored higher on measures of authoritarianism (see Chapter 3) than those from the North.[26] What this means is that individual bigotry is only *part* of the explanation of racial discrimination: *conformity with social norms*, according to which discrimination is not just accepted but often expected, can prove an even more powerful determinant of prejudiced behaviour than stereotyped beliefs and hostile feelings. (For more examples of conformity and other environmental influences, see Chapter 4.)

DEHUMANIZATION AND INFRAHUMANIZATION

The following account of *dehumanization* and *infrahumanization* spans the three components of prejudiced attitudes that we've been discussing: they refer to ways of thinking and feeling about outgroups, which can then be used to justify discrimination in its various forms, including genocide.

To begin with some examples, (i) victims of genocide are labelled as vermin by the perpetrators; (ii) slaves are officially rated as worth a fraction of a person; (iii) immigrants are likened to invasive pests or infectious diseases; (iv) monkey chants and bananas are aimed at black footballers in European football stadia; (v) sex offenders are called animals.[27]

History is filled with examples of *dehumanization*. In Ancient Greece, Barbarians were strangers unable to speak Greek but considered (almost) equals; but with increasing slavery and the expanding Roman Empire, Barbarians came to be seen as stupid, dangerous and living like animals. Explorers, scientists, anthropologists (such as Levi-Strauss and Sumner) have always noted that people glorify their own groups while vilifying strangers (the 'other').

However, social psychology has only recently started to investigate why it's so difficult to grant equal humanness to all human beings. Psychological research has shown that dehumanization is a pervasive phenomenon in interpersonal and intergroup contexts, occurring in a wide variety of social domains.[28]

> Dehumanization is important as a psychological phenomenon because it can be so common and yet so dire in its consequences. It is the most striking violation of our belief in a common humanity: our Enlightenment assumption that we are all essentially one and the same.[29]

'*Infrahumanization*' was coined to describe a more subtle form of dehumanization: while 'dehumanization' implies an *absolute* denial of humanness, infrahumanization implies *relative* differences. It's a form of ethnocentrism in which ingroups reserve the 'human essence' for themselves: outgroups are something *less* than human.[30] Specifically, infrahumanization involves attributing fewer *secondary* (or 'refined') *emotions* to outgroup members than to ingroup members; these are uniquely human emotions ('*sentiments*' in French), such as hope and remorse, in contrast with *primary* emotions – such as anger and fear – that humans share with other species.

> Infrahumanization theory was a major theoretical advance. It recognized that humanness can be denied to others in subtle and commonplace ways, rather than being confined to blatant

denials in killing fields and torture chambers. It provided a clear operational definition of humanness as those attributes that distinguish humans from other animals.[31]

THE DUAL MODEL OF DEHUMANIZATION

According to the *dual model of dehumanization* (DMD),[32] human uniqueness and the human/animal distinction it rests on is only one of the ways of understanding humanness. We also tend to conceptualize humanness by opposing it to robots and automatons. In *'animalistic'* dehumanization, individuals are denied *human uniqueness*: they lack refinement, self-control, intelligence and rationality. In *'mechanistic'* dehumanization, individuals are denied *human nature*: they lack warmth, emotion and individuality

The DMD represents an extension of infrahumanization theory. It aims to account for the diverse forms of dehumanization – subtle or blatant, animal – or object-related, intergroup or interpersonal – rather than picking out a specific phenomenon in group perception.[33]

STEREOTYPE CONTENT MODEL

A third theoretical account defines dehumanization as the failure to spontaneously consider another person's mind or to engage in social cognition when perceiving them. The *stereotype content model* (SCM) identifies two key dimensions, *warmth* (friendliness, trustworthiness) and *competence* (capability, assertiveness), as predicting the key content of stereotypes, as well as our emotional responses to different individuals and groups; in turn, these emotions predict the sorts of target most likely to be dehumanized.[34]

Ingroups are perceived as *high* on both dimensions, pitied groups (such as the elderly) are seen as high on warmth but low on competence, envied groups (e.g. the wealthy) are seen as cold but competent, and groups that evoke disgust (e.g. the homeless) are seen as *low* on both. Dehumanizing perceptions target these 'lowest of the low'; these groups consistently fail to engage the network in the brain that underpins social cognition (the 'social cognition network', namely, the medial prefrontal cortex and superior temporal sulcus) and instead activate disgust-related structures (such as the insula; see Chapter 2). These groups also fail to elicit spontaneous attributions of mental states compared to high-high (e.g. citizens, middle class, Americans, Canadians, Christians), high-low (elderly, disabled, children, Italians, Irish) or low-high groups (rich, professional, technical experts, Asians, Jewish people, British, Germans).[35] Cold but incompetent groups may also be dehumanized as robot-like, consistent with the mechanistic form.[36]

While the elderly, for example (high-low) evoke pity and sympathy, Americans (high-high) evoke pride and admiration and the wealthy, envy, jealousy and resentment. In addition to the homeless, the poor, immigrants, Latinos, Africans and Muslims evoke disgust and contempt.[37] (See Table 1.1.)

Table 1.1 Persistent warmth and competence stereotypes commonly found in the U.S., with the emotions they typically evoke (based on Fiske, 2018)

	Low competence (capability, assertiveness)	High competence (capability, assertiveness)
High warmth (friendliness, trustworthiness)	1 Elderly. Disabled. Children. United States. Italians. Irish. **Emotions evoked**: pity, sympathy	2 Citizens. Middle Class. Defaults. United States. Americans. Canadians. Christians. **Emotions evoked**: pride, admiration
Low warmth (friendliness, trustworthiness)	3 Poor. Homeless. Immigrants. United States. Latinos. Africans. Muslims. **Emotions evoked**: disgust, contempt	4 Rich. Professional. Technical Experts. United States. Asians. Jews. British. Germans. **Emotions evoked**: envy, jealousy, resentment

Research has identified an ever-growing list of groups that have been the targets of dehumanization, including lower socioeconomic groups, those with mental disorders (or 'the mentally ill'), violent criminals and asexual people.[38] When women's bodies are sexualized or made visually salient, they're attributed with less mind, moral worth, competence and capacity to experience pain. Sexualized women are visually processed as objects rather than people,[39] and hostile sexist men viewing sexualized images of women showed reduced neural activation in social cognition networks.[40] Sexualized women are implicitly associated with animals by both male and female perceivers.[41] Women are more likely to be dehumanized if seen drinking alcohol or in an alcohol-related context, and the more alcohol a woman is believed to have consumed, the greater the degree of dehumanization. What links these two things is her perceived sexual availability.[42]

EXPLICIT VERSUS IMPLICIT DEHUMANIZATION: ARE WE ALL RACISTS?

We began this section with some examples of what may be called *explicit* or blatant dehumanization ('reducing' people to vermin etc.). We have also seen how infrahumanization represents a more subtle, more *implicit* form of dehumanization. An even more subtle form of dehumanization is the *implicit associations* people hold about social groups, i.e. ways of thinking that they aren't consciously aware of.

Most of us would (strongly) deny that we are racially, sexually or in any other way prejudiced. But what we probably understand by this claim is 'old-fashioned', *explicit*, overt, blatant, crude racist etc. discrimination (as in anti-locution: see earlier); this now constitutes a form of 'hate crime' (at least in the U.K.).[43] But what about *modern*,[44] *symbolic*[45] or *aversive racism*?[46]

'Modern', 'symbolic' and 'aversive' describe attitudes of the political liberal who openly endorses egalitarianism. While a majority of white Americans appear non-prejudiced on self-report (*explicit*) measures such as the Modern Racism Scale (MRS)[47] and the Symbolic

Racism Scale (SRS),[48] is it possible that they harbour *unconscious* negative beliefs or feelings that are expressed in subtle, indirect, implicit ways?[49] Psychologists have found evidence for such a discrepancy.[50]

In one such study,[51] white participants reported very low self-perceived racial bias on the MRS. While in a functional magnetic resonance imaging scanner (fMRI), and before completing the MRS, they were shown pictures of either black or white male faces (all strangers with neutral facial expressions), one at a time; they had to decide whether it was the same face as the last or a different one. The researchers' focus was on the *amygdala*, a brain structure implicated in processing threat and detecting socially important stimuli.

Participants were also given the Implicit Association Test (IAT);[52] this is presented on a computer and comprises several stages: (i) 'black/bad' appears in the top left corner of the screen, and 'white/good' in the top right corner; (ii) single names (e.g. 'Temeka') are then presented in the centre of the screen: the participant has to decide whether to categorize the name as 'black' or 'white'; similarly, whether words (e.g. 'wonderful') are 'good' or 'bad'; (iii) the categories are then reversed: 'black/good' and 'white/bad'.

The researchers used *reaction time* to measure bias: if participants classify 'wonderful' as 'good' faster with 'white/good' than with 'black/good' on the screen, then they are judged to be displaying an *implicit, anti-black bias* (or *pro-white bias*). This was, indeed, what was found.

When the IAT results were compared with the imaging data, it was found that the higher the pro-white bias, the greater the amygdala activation in response to black versus white faces. Interestingly, this pro-white bias disappeared when participants were shown a mix of faces of famous people (including Muhammad Ali, Denzel Washington, Harrison Ford and John F. Kennedy).

The IAT has become arguably the most famous and widely taken modern psychological test.[53] However, serious concerns have been raised over both its *reliability* (take the test today and again tomorrow and you'll probably get different scores) and *validity* (what it actually measures). Its designers originally claimed that it measures levels of unconscious social biases and their tendency to act in a discriminatory way.[54] However, they now admit that this second claim cannot be defended.[55] If the IAT really does measure implicit prejudice and predict discriminatory behaviour, then it should be possible to mediate changes in explicit bias or overt behaviour by reducing the implicit bias. However, there's very little evidence to support this claim.[56]

Unconscious states are notoriously difficult to identify; associations between words and categories may simply be measuring familiar cultural or linguistic affiliations (e.g. associating 'blue' and 'sky' faster than 'blue' and 'doughnuts' doesn't mean that you're unconsciously prejudiced against cakes). Also, negative words have more emotive salience than positive words, so the IAT may be tapping into this negativity bias rather than prejudice.[57]

While we're more likely to deny being prejudiced on a self-report (explicit) measure than we used to be, and despite the more subtle nature of infrahumanization, blatant dehumanization is still all too prevalent. Across several online surveys, hundreds of U.S. and U.K. participants were asked a host of attitudinal questions and asked to rate different ethnic groups on how evolved they are, using a graphic depicting the famous 'Ascent of Man' (which shows a chimpanzee, followed by a hunched but upright ape, followed by a more upright human-like figure and finally 'modern man'). By setting a slider somewhere between the two ends, participants could designate ethnic groups as being less than human.[58]

Initial results using this 'Ascent scale' found that the U.S. participants dehumanize Arabs and Muslims the most; a weaker but similar pattern was found for South Koreans and Mexican people. The degree of dehumanization of Arabs was correlated with the participants' desire for reducing Arab immigration, lack of sympathy towards an unjustly treated delinquent teen of Arab ethnicity and endorsement of acts of violence, such as advocating torture or bombing an entire Arab country.

This way of measuring dehumanization seems to be particularly useful when the ingroup feels under direct threat of violence. In the two weeks following the Boston Marathon bombings in 2013, U.S.

participants showed significantly greater Arab dehumanization compared with data collected two months before. Again, this was a strong
predictor of many of the attitudes listed earlier and of agreement with
extreme tweets, such as one advocating that all Muslims be wiped off
the face of the earth. Similar results were found for U.K. participants
following the brutal murder of Lee Rigby, the off-duty British soldier,
also in 2013: high dehumanization was correlated with support for
drone strikes, punitive treatment of the perpetrators and aggressive
counterterrorism policy against Arabs and Muslims. Compared with
measures of infrahumanization, blatant dehumanization, as measured by the Ascent scale, seems to better capture our state of mind in
volatile contexts.

> In an age where nationalism and ethnic identity are returning
> to the political centre-stage – from the rise of the European far-
> right to the emergence of the so-called Islamic State which treats
> those unlike themselves as non-human – it's important that we
> are able to measure and understand this treatment of 'the other'.[59]

CONCLUSIONS: WHO DEFINES WHAT'S 'HUMAN'?

If there's an 'opposite' of dehumanizing (members of) an outgroup,
it's perceiving all ingroups and outgroups as belonging to the same,
superordinate, all-inclusive 'humanity' (or 'human beings'), sharing
the same set of psychological traits and characteristics. 'We all have one
fundamental thing in common, namely, we are all human' is surely
the ultimate antidote to dehumanization and infrahumanization.

While this might be fine in theory, it implicitly assumes that all
in- and outgroups would define 'human' in the same way. But is this
the case?

There's considerable cross-cultural agreement about the defining
features of human beings, or what makes humans unique. For example, a study involving Polish, Japanese and Scottish students found
that the same emotions (e.g. admiration, compassion, disenchant-
ment, melancholy, nostalgia) are perceived as uniquely human in

these three different cultures, while others (e.g. fear, pain, sorrow, affection) are seen as being shared with other species.[60] These correspond to the secondary and primary emotions, respectively, which are distinguished within infrahumanization that we discussed earlier. Secondary emotions emerge in later stages of development, are socially learned and involve more cognitive and moral processing than do the primary ('animalistic') emotions.[61]

But is there more to humanity than secondary emotions?

Another cross-cultural study performed in Australia, China and Italy showed that secondary emotion and *higher cognitive abilities* (thinking skills) are perceived as distinguishing humans from animals, while any emotional life (both primary and secondary emotions) and *free will* (wishes, intentions) are perceived as distinguishing humans from robots.[62] So 'human uniqueness' and 'human nature' are similar but not identical.[63]

While there's considerable cross-cultural agreement regarding human uniqueness, there's much less agreement about the extent to which people of different 'races', classes or ethnicities display it. Each group member perceives his/her own group as *more human* than other groups,[64] and each individual perceives him/herself as more human than other people.[65]

Mirroring these cross-cultural differences is the finding that majority groups tend to perceive minorities as *less prototypical* of the society they belong to; in terms of the superordinate category 'human being', the ingroup regards outgroups as possessing less 'humanness' than itself. This leads directly to negative intergroup emotions and prejudice against immigrants.[66]

Exclusion from humanity also has a geographical dimension, as it is related to distance from outgroup members. For example, citizens of former colonial empires dehumanize members of colonialized nations, attributing them with fewer secondary emotions when they learn about ingroup involvement in historical colonial atrocities.[67] What this tells us is that dehumanization becomes a strategy of *moral disengagement*: outgroup members can retrospectively justify/rationalize their past atrocities by re-defining the victims as less than human, and so the atrocities don't 'count' as they would if they themselves had been the victims.

A content analysis of The New York Times, Wall Street Journal and New York Post found that descriptions of an ingroup-targeting disaster (Hurricane Katrina) included significantly more secondary emotion words compared with descriptions of the Asian tsunami, an outgroup-targeting disaster.[68] Other studies have found that white people attributed fewer secondary emotions to the black victims of Hurricane Katrina – and vice versa. This lack of shared humanity was found to be generally responsible for not going to the aid of other people.[69] It seems that black and white victims of a 'shared' disaster don't define themselves and each other as belonging to the superordinate category of 'victimhood'.[70]

2

PREJUDICE WITHIN BIOLOGY, PSYCHOLOGY AND PSYCHIATRY

THE CONCEPT OF 'RACE': HOW DID IT ORIGINATE?

Some of the first known uses of the term date from the 16th century, when it referred to a group of people from common stock, like a family, tribe or – at a stretch – a small nation. Even up to the 18th-century European Enlightenment, many still saw physical differences as a shifting thing, rooted in geography: if people in hotter climates with dark skin moved somewhere colder, their skin colour would automatically lighten.[1]

The notion of 'race' as hard and fixed emerged slowly, largely from Enlightenment science. Swedish botanist Carl Linnaeus, famous for classifying the natural world, in the tenth edition of *Systema Naturae* (1758), identified four main 'flavours' of human: red, white, yellow and black, corresponding, respectively, to the Americas, Europe, Asia and Africa. These 'races' quickly became slotted into hierarchies based on the politics of the time, character becoming confused with appearance and political circumstance becoming biological fact. For example, Linnaeus described Native Americans ('Red Indians') as 'subjugated', as though this was in their nature.[2]

By the 19th century, the possibility that 'races' existed and some were inferior to others gave European *colonialism* 'a moral kick in the drive for public support'.[3] Similarly, in the U.S. perception of the natives of colonized countries as too uncivilized and barbaric to matter was used to justify *slavery*. Even after death, slaves were financially valuable, their bodies being sold for medical research:

> It's ironic that much of our modern scientific understanding of human anatomy was built on the bodies of those who were considered at the time to be less than human.[4]
>
> In place of universal humanity came a self-serving version of the human story, in which racial difference became an excuse for treating people differently. Time and again, *science* provided the intellectual authority for racism, just as it had helped define race to begin with.[5]

Myth and science coexisted, and both served politics. In the run-up to passage of the 13th Amendment in 1865, abolishing slavery in the U.S., the 'race question' wasn't resolved – it just became thornier. Although many Americans believed in emancipation on *moral* grounds, many believed that full equality wasn't achievable because black people weren't *biologically* equal; even Jefferson and Lincoln believed that they were inherently inferior.[6]

DARWIN, EVOLUTION AND 'RACE'

Back in the U.K., Charles Darwin's *On the Origin of Species by Means of Natural Selection* was published in 1859.[7] Although it dealt almost exclusively with the evolution of plants and animals, a fierce debate quickly ensued over its implication regarding human beings (largely ignored by Darwin himself): Are we God's special creation, or are we 'descended from the apes'? Support for the latter view, which, of course, was Darwin's preference, initially came mainly from the English biologist Thomas Henry Huxley (an expert on primate anatomy). This, together with discovery of the skulls and stuffed bodies of gorillas in 1861 (previously unknown to Western science) and other fossil finds, helped make evolutionary theory widely accepted within the scientific community.

Three later seminal works directly addressed the evolution of human beings, the most relevant to 'race' being *The Descent of Man and Selection in Relation to Sex* in 1871.[8] In it, Darwin claimed that human beings are descended from animal ancestors. But he argues that 'there is no fundamental difference between man and the higher mammals in their mental faculties';[9] for example, dogs clearly experience many of the same emotions as humans, including jealousy, pride, shame and even a rudimentary sense of humour.[10] Animals also demonstrate memory, attention, curiosity and even imagination (based on their apparent dreaming) and basic *reason* (as indicated by their ability to learn from experience and communicate with each other). Darwin concluded that 'The difference in mind between man and the higher animals, great as it is, certainly is one of degree and not kind'.[11]

The Victorian era in Britain was characterized by extreme views regarding 'race' and the causes of ethnic differences.[12] According to the *polygenists*, non-European 'savage' peoples represented a distinctly different *species* of being, while the *monogenists* believed in the common ancestry and relatedness of all human groups. However, the monogenists also proposed widely varying explanations of racial differences, ranging from cultural/environmental to a belief in descent from Noah's son Ham.

Darwin clearly fell into the monogenist camp. *The Descent of Man* swept away the religious creation myths and framed the human species as having had one common ancestor many millennia ago, evolving slowly like all life on earth. He stressed the similarity of basic bodily responses, concluding that we could only have evolved from shared origins; human races didn't emerge separately.

However, Darwin also argued that environmental and educational factors were extremely influential in producing individual differences, with slavery, in particular, having horrible effects on its victims. The widely varying environmental conditions experienced by different groups would inevitably create differing *selection pressures* among them: such pressures might help account for the evolution, over time, of slightly different 'races' (or 'sub-species'),[13] as in the case of dark skin colour being a natural adaptation to more direct exposure to sunlight. While this may in itself be a perfectly 'innocent' account of racial differences:

> An elaboration of this theory held that the struggle for survival in harsh northern climates promoted the development of inventiveness and creativity and accounted for a presumed intellectual superiority of the so-called Nordic [Northern European] races.[14]

While human beings as a whole constitute a 'species' with fertile mating within it, each 'sub-species' is *partially isolated reproductively* from the others.[15] According to this model, Nordics and Africans, for example, have maintained their distinctiveness because mating occurred predominantly within each population. Although this view of 'race' as a sub-species promoted the concept of 'geographical race', it didn't *exclude* the view that 'races' may become separate types: a sub-species may evolve to the point where it's no longer *able* to interbreed with other sub-species.

This idea was more strongly supported by some of Darwin's contemporaries and followers than by Darwin himself – although he never explicitly refuted it. Indeed, he was ambivalent regarding whether black Africans and Australians were strictly equal to white Europeans on the evolutionary scale. Populations may have diverged since the time of the common ancestor, producing levels of difference. He saw gradations between 'the highest men of the highest races and the lowest savages'; e.g. 'children of savages' have a stronger tendency to protrude their lips when they sulk than European children, because they are closer to the 'primordial condition', similar to chimps. Without apparent embarrassment, Darwin believed in an *evolutionary hierarchy*: men were above women, white races above others.

In *The Descent of Man*, Darwin seemed to have succumbed to the mood of his times, wherein it was argued by some that brown and yellow races were a bit higher up than black, while whites were the most evolved and, by implication, the most civilized and most human. The success of white races became couched in the language of 'survival of the fittest': the most 'primitive' peoples (or 'savage races') would likely become extinct because of their inability to change habits when brought into contact with 'civilized races'. He then joined his cousin Francis Galton in calling for *eugenic* measures to maintain the integrity of the latter (see the discussion of eugenics in what follows).[16]

Some of Darwin's supporters were fervent racists, including Huxley ('Darwin's Bulldog'; whites are 'bigger-brained') and the German zoologist Ernst Haeckel, who saw black Africans as a kind of 'missing link' in the evolutionary chain that connected apes to white Europeans.[17] Indeed, compared with those of his contemporaries, Darwin's view was flexible and egalitarian.[18] For example, Robert Knox, a doctor and teacher of medical students at Edinburgh, was a strong and extremely influential propagandist for racial theories in Britain.[19] In *The Races of Men*, he maintained that external characteristics (mainly skin colour) reflected internal ones (such as intelligence and capacity for cultural pursuits): dark races were generally inferior, and 'hybrids' ('mixed-race') were eventually sterile. The view of 'race' as a human type had been taken to an extreme in order to produce the concept of human kind being divisible into 'pure' races that don't mix.[20]

One other physical characteristic that was taken as the basis for racial classification is the cranium (skull). Morton, an 19th-century American doctor and 'craniometrist', studied the volume of craniums collected from all over the world. He claimed that people could be divided into five races, representing separate acts of creation: whites/Caucasians are the most intelligent; then East Asians ('Mongolian'); then Southeast Asians, Native Americans and finally blacks ('Ethiopians'). Each race had its own distinct character, corresponding to their place in a divinely determined hierarchy.

In the decades before the American Civil War (1861–1865), Morton's ideas were quickly adopted by defenders of slavery, and today, he's widely regarded as the father of *scientific racism*.[21]

THE CURRENT STATUS OF THE 'RACE' CONCEPT

POST-WORLD WAR II DEVELOPMENTS

In 1949, more than 100 scientists, anthropologists, diplomats and international policy makers met in Paris under the umbrella of

UNESCO (United Nations Educational, Scientific and Cultural Organization) to redefine 'race'. British-born American anthropologist Ashley Montagu led the charge against *scientific racism* and its horrific legacy; he took his cue from a wave of social scientists who'd already long argued that history, culture and environment were really behind what people thought of as 'racial difference'.[22]

In *Man's Most Dangerous Myth; The Fallacy of Race*,[23] Montagu claimed that 'The word race is itself racist'. Humans are likely to be genetically almost identical, and, in any case, our ancestral roots were certainly the same. As anthropologists and geneticists were learning, individual variations *within* populations were at least as great as *between* populations (see Lewontin in what follows), making racial boundaries impossible to draw: each so-called 'race' blurs into the next. What makes people and nations seem different are culture and language.

UNESCO published its first statement on 'race' in 1950: it stressed unity between humans (we all belong to the same species, *Homo sapiens*) and aimed to remove racism once and for all.

> This marked a crucial moment in history, a bold universal attempt to reverse the deep-seated damage done by racism – and perpetuated by science – for at least two centuries. Whether we realised it or not, all of us thought about race differently after that. Racism was no longer acceptable.[24]

But not everyone agreed, and in 1951 UNESCO gathered a team of experts to publish a new statement, tempering its language to account for the lack of consensus around the biological facts. It had to make clear that not every expert could accept even the most basic fact that we all belong to the same species.

However, by this time, 'race' was being studied within the social sciences, cultural studies and history (as distinct from biology). It was understood to be a social and political *construction* – not borne out of biology. New institutes dedicated to the study of human variation began to open all over the world, describing 'populations' and 'ethnic groups' instead of 'races'. However, racial categories still lived in people's minds, in everyday life, playing out in the politics and racism of the real world.[25]

One of the new ways of continuing to study racial differences was blood type. In the 1960s, the WHO (World Health Organization) launched its own effort to document groups of people around the world, collecting data on skin pigmentation and hair form, blood type, colour blindness and other genetic markers. At least some scientists were searching for proof that 'race' was genetically tangible, that evidence for deep racial differences could be found at the molecular level.

A landmark paper by geneticist Lewontin[26] explored the true breadth of human biological diversity. Comparing seven human groups based roughly on old-fashioned racial categories, he concluded that around 85 per cent of all genetic diversity is found within local populations and another 8 per cent if you compare continental populations. In total, around 90 per cent of the variation lies within the old racial categories. Today's geneticists overwhelmingly agree with him.

Humans are a relatively new species, so we're still closely related to one another. The greatest genetic diversity within our species is found inside Africa – this continent contains the oldest human communities. When some began to migrate 50,000 to 100,000 years ago, these were genetically less diverse than the remainers – the former were composed of fewer people. The human variation we see across regions today is partly a result of this 'founder effect'. As these migrants spread, bred and adapted to their local environments, they began to look more different from the remaining relatives and more like each other. This happened each time new migrants left for new territory.[27]

Twentieth-century genetics at first described different 'races' in terms of blood types, but this proved unreliable. More recently, scientific advances have enabled geneticists to identify human genes that code for specific enzymes and other proteins. But the genetic differences between the classically described races (European, Indian, African, East Asian, New World and Oceanian) are, on average, only slightly higher (10 per cent) than those that exist between nations *within* a racial group (6 per cent), and the genetic differences between individuals within a population are *far greater* than either of these (84 per cent).[28]

'Race' defined as 'genetically discrete groups' *doesn't* exist.[29] Nevertheless, the traditional view persists that people resembling each other in obvious ways belong to a 'race' that represents a genetically distinct human type. Anthropologists, biologists and those in medicine are all guilty of perpetuating this myth, despite the widely held belief that 'race' has lost its scientific meaning. For example, two people of *different* 'races' can have more genes in common than two 'members' of the *same* race.[30]

Geneticists now believe that the whole concept of 'race' is misconceived: when the first complete human genome was assembled (in 2000), it was declared that the concept of 'race' has no genetic/scientific basis. However, genetic research over recent decades has revealed two deep truths about people:

1 All humans are closely related – more so than all chimpanzees (even though there are many more humans than chimpanzees). We all have the same collection of genes, but (with the exception of identical or monozygotic/MZ twins) with slightly different versions of them.
2 Based on studies of this genetic diversity, scientists have reconstructed a sort of family tree of human populations: in a very real sense, all people alive today are Africans.

ETHNIC DIVERSITY AND SKIN COLOUR

The Khoe-San (of South Africa) represent one of the oldest branches of the human family tree; the Pygmies (of central Africa) also have a very long history as a separate group. This means that the deepest splits in the human family *aren't* between, say, whites or blacks or Asians or Native Americans; rather, they're between African populations such as the Khoe-San and Pygmies, who spent tens of thousands of years separated from one another even before humans left Africa.[31] There's greater diversity in Africa than on all other continents combined; that's because modern humans originated there and have lived there the longest, providing them with time to evolve enormous genetic diversity, including skin colour (and its 2,000-plus languages are used as a guide). There is no homogeneous African 'race'; those who left Africa 60,000 years ago reflected only a fraction of Africa's diversity.[32] As one geneticist puts it:

> There are 1.3 billion Africans, 42 million African Americans. Not only are these huge numbers, but the people in question are more diverse genetically than anyone else on Earth. And yet westerners refer to all of them as 'black'. This is a scientifically meaningless classification, and one that is baked into western culture from five centuries of scientific racism. Stereotyping based on pigmentation is foolish, because racial differences are skin deep.[33]

'Race' is a *social*, not a biological, category.[34] Similarly:

> 'Race' is a social rather than a natural phenomenon, a process which gives significance to superficial physical differences, but where the construction of group divisions depends [on] . . . economic, political and cultural processes.[35]

Many writers prefer to put quotation marks around 'race' (as I have often done here) to indicate that we're dealing with one possible social classification of people and groups rather than an established biological/genetic 'reality'.[36]

EUGENICS

As noted earlier, Darwin joined his younger cousin, biologist Francis Galton, in calling for *eugenic* measures to maintain the integrity of the 'civilized races'. 'Eugenics' (from the Greek '*eu*' meaning 'well'/'good') refers to the idea of using social control to improve the health/intelligence of future generations. Galton, widely recognized as the 'father' of eugenics, drew on Darwin's theory of evolution by natural selection, according to which individuals in a population show a wide variety of characteristics: those with characteristics most suited to their environment will survive and breed, passing on those beneficial traits. A 'race' of people could be more quickly improved if the most intelligent were encouraged to reproduce, while the most stupid would be discouraged/prevented from doing so.

HOW WOULD THIS WORK?

The first challenge was to measure people's abilities, to build up a data bank about exactly who were the most and least intelligent. In 1904, Galton convinced University College London (UCL) to set up the world's first Eugenics Record Office, dedicated to measuring human differences, in the hope of understanding what kind of people Great Britain might want more of. This became known as the Galton Laboratory of National Eugenics. (Long after his death, it was renamed the Department of Genetics, Evolution & Environment, housed in the Darwin Building. Galton collaborated closely with the mathematician Karl Pearson, who, after Galton's death, became the first professor of national eugenics in 1911.)

Despite Galton's expeditions to Africa and his encounters with other cultures, he failed to see their common humanity; if anything, his racist assumptions were reinforced ('savage races'). His racism combined with his obsession with measuring things; through eugenics, he saw a way of using what he thought he knew about human difference, shored up by Darwin's theory of natural selection, to systematically improve the quality of the 'British race'. If we are animals, then we can be improved through selective breeding. His work is fundamental to the story of *scientific racism*: he's part of the way we invented racism and how we think about it.[37]

Eugenics reduces human beings to their genetic inheritance (*genetic determinism*). In the early 1900s, before the advent of modern genetics, Galton's ideas seemed to make sense to many. While today we associate eugenics with the Nazi movement, it had a logical appeal that crossed the political spectrum; before the 1930s, many on the left saw it as socially progressive. Galton was a fellow of the Royal Society and was supported by the British Medical Association (BMA). 'Eugenics belonged firmly to establishment science, and . . . wasn't just mainstream, it was fashionable'.[38]

HOW COULD EUGENICS ACHIEVE ITS GOALS?

Central to eugenics is managing reproduction. To support her first birth control clinic, Marie Stopes, women's rights activist and birth control pioneer, founded the Society for Constructive Birth Control and Racial Progress. Philosopher Bertrand Russell suggested the state might improve the health of the population by fining the 'wrong' type of people for giving birth.

Winston Churchill was welcomed as vice president of the first International Eugenics Congress held in London in 1912. Indiana had already passed the world's first involuntary sterilization law in 1907: eugenicists argued that criminality, mental disorders and poverty were hereditary. More than 30 other U.S. states soon followed. By 1910, the Eugenics Record Office had been set up in New York; one of its aims was 'the study of *miscegenation* in the U.S.' (the mixing and intermarriage of different racial groups). The hardware behind at least one of America's most ambitious eugenics projects came from IBM, which went on to supply the Nazi regime with the technology needed to transport millions of Jews and other minorities to the concentration camps.[39]

In the first decades of the 20th century, all over the world, eugenics began to be conflated with 19th-century ideas about 'race'. For example, European notions of racial superiority were mirrored in India's existing *caste system* – itself a kind of racial hierarchy – and Germany's Aryan myth placed the noble race as having once lived in India. The ideological quest for the true 'Aryans' remains alive in India and *Mein Kampf* is a bestseller there.[40]

While early, mainstream eugenics focused on improving racial stock by weeding out the feeble-minded, insane and disabled, over time its reach expanded. Pearson argued that intermixing superior (white) and other (non-white) 'races' endangered the former's health: the very existence of those other 'races' represented a threat. Uncontrolled immigration threatened the welfare of British people. Despite the pressure put on it by eugenicists such as Pearson, the British government never implemented eugenics.

However, the situation in the U.S. was dramatically different. The Chinese Exclusion Act (1882) was its first major law restricting immigration. This was followed, as noted earlier, by Indiana's involuntary sterilization law in 1907, the world's first and the first of a majority of other states. The 1924 Restriction Act reflected the lobbying of eugenicists, who not only wanted limits to immigration but also wanted to impose harsh quotas against nations of 'inferior stock' (namely, East and South European nations). The eugenicists battled and won one of the greatest victories of scientific racism in U.S. history: 'America must be kept American', proclaimed President Coolidge as he signed the bill.[41]

These quotas stood and slowed immigration from southern and eastern Europe to a trickle. Throughout the 1930s, Jewish refugees, anticipating the Holocaust, sought to emigrate but were refused admission – even when quotas from western and northern Europe weren't filled. Estimates suggest that up to 6 million southern, central and eastern Europeans were barred between 1924 and 1939.

> We know what happened to many who wished to leave but had nowhere to go. The paths to destruction are often indirect, but ideas can be agents as sure as guns and bombs.[42]

Only in 1974 did Indiana repeal legislation that had made it legal to sterilize those considered undesirable. However, it was revealed in 2013 that doctors working for the California Department of Corrections & Rehabilitation had continued sterilizing as many as 150 female inmates between 2006 and 2010, possibly by coercing them.

In Japan, a 1948 Eugenic Protection Law to sterilize those with mental disorder and physical disabilities and so prevent the birth of 'inferior' offspring was only repealed in 1996. Victims are still fighting for justice.[43]

PSYCHOLOGY, EUGENICS AND INTELLIGENCE TESTING

A major 'scientific' weapon that the American eugenicists used in their ultimately successful fight for the Restriction Act was the outcome of mass intelligence testing of World War I Army recruits (the 'Army data'). But in order to appreciate this phenomenon, we need to consider what took place in France earlier in the century.

In 1904, Alfred Binet, a French psychologist, was commissioned by the French minister of public education to develop a method for identifying those children who might need some form of special education. The result was a collection of short tasks, related to everyday life problems, which are widely recognized as the first formal test of intelligence (1905). Initially, intelligence was calculated as chronological age (CA) minus mental age (MA); children whose MA was sufficiently behind their CA could then be recommended for special education. However, it was pointed out that division is more appropriate than subtraction: it's the relative (not the absolute) size of the difference that matters; hence the intelligence quotient (IQ) was now defined as $MA/CA \times 100/1$.[44]

H.H. Goddard introduced Binet's intelligence scales to the U.S., advocating their use (and translating Binet's articles into English). Goddard agreed with Binet that the scale worked best in identifying children just below the normal range. But whereas Binet refused to label IQ as a measure of innate, general intelligence that could be used to rank all pupils, Goddard regarded IQ as just that: his purpose in using the scales was (i) to recognize people's limits so that they could be segregated (to label in order to limit) and (ii) to curtail breeding so as to prevent further decline of the American 'stock', which was already threatened by immigration from without and by the prolific reproduction of the feeble-minded from within. This first aim is what differentiates strict *hereditarians* (or *genetic theorists*) from their opponents (Binet's aim was to identify those children who needed help to *improve*),[45] and the second marks Goddard out as a *eugenicist*. Hereditarians also believe that IQ differences are largely determined by fixed biological (i.e. genetic) differences between people.

> The IQ test can be regarded as an ideological weapon, used by white-dominated society to oppress minority groups, especially (but by no means exclusively) African Americans and people of African-Caribbean origin in the U.K. As scientists, psychologists responsible for the construction and use of IQ tests are meant, and are seen by society at large, to be objective and value-free. However . . . their theories and instruments have too often been dangerous reflections of their own personal motives and racial, class and sexual prejudices.[46]

Robert Yerkes, another American hereditarian and eugenicist, wanted to show that psychology could be as rigorous a science as physics, involving measurement and quantification. *Psychometrics* (mental measurement), as illustrated by Binet's IQ test, promised to help Yerkes achieve his goal. With the approach of World War I, Yerkes's 'big idea' was to persuade the U.S. Army to test *all* its recruits; he successfully campaigned, within both the government and the psychology profession, and, as Colonel Yerkes, he supervised the testing of 1.75 million recruits between 1914 and 1918. Together with Goddard and Lewis Terman (who standardized Binet's test for use in the U.S., subsequently known as the Stanford-Binet test), he constructed two new army mental tests during 1917:[47]

- The *Army Alpha* test was designed for literate recruits and comprised an eight-part written exam, taking less than an hour. Large numbers could be tested at one time.
- The seven-part *Army Beta* test was designed for illiterate recruits and those who failed the Army Alpha. It comprised a *pictorial* test, including numbers and symbols.

Those who failed the Army Beta would be recalled for an individual exam. Psychologists would then grade each man from A to E (with pluses and minuses) and recommend appropriate military placement.

According to Yerkes, the tests measured 'native intellectual ability', that is, ability that's unaffected by environmental factors, such as acquired knowledge, education and life experience. The absurdity of such a claim is illustrated by questions such as the following:

- Crisco is a: patent medicine, disinfectant, toothpaste, food product?
- Christy Mathewson is famous as a: writer, artist, baseball player, comedian?

Clearly, the answers depend on *knowledge* – not innate ability!

There was considerable inconsistency between Army camps regarding their ability to follow the protocol (i.e. allocating men to the appropriate test), which created a systematic bias that substantially lowered the mean (average) scores of African Americans and immigrants. Many took only Alpha and scored either zero or close to zero, not because they were innately stupid but because they were illiterate and should have taken Beta. How did this happen?

Recruits and draftees had, on average, spent fewer years in school than Yerkes had anticipated; this meant that provision for taking Beta became unmanageable. Also, given the time pressure and hostility of regular officers, the protocol hardly applied to African Americans, who, as usual, were treated with less concern and more contempt: while 50 per cent scored D- on Beta, only 20 per cent were recalled for an individual exam. When the protocol was followed, their scores improved dramatically.[48]

Scores from 160,000 cases of Alpha, Beta and individual exams were converted to a common standard so that racial and national averages could be calculated.[49] Three 'facts' emerged from this exercise, which continued to influence U.S. social policy long after their source had been forgotten:

1 The average MA of white American adults was a shocking 13 – just above the edge of *moronity*. (Goddard had earlier used

'morons' – from the Greek for foolish – to describe those with a MA of 8–12.) Terman had previously set the standard at 16. This new figure became a rallying point for eugenicists, who mourned the decline of American intelligence, caused by the unconstrained interbreeding of the poor and feeble-minded, the spread of 'Negro blood' through interbreeding and the swamping of an intelligent native stock by the 'immigrating dregs of southern and eastern Europe'.[50]

2 European immigrants could be graded by their country of origin. The average man of several nations was a moron. The darker people of southern Europe and the Slavs of eastern Europe were less intelligent than the fair people of western and northern Europe. The average Russian had an MA of 11.34, the Italian 11.01 and the Pole 10.74.

3 The Negro lay at the bottom, with an average MA of 10.41. Some camps divided black people into three groups based on the intensity of their skin colour; not surprisingly, the lighter groups scored higher.

These figures for racial and national differences gave hereditarians license to claim that the fact and extent of group differences in innate intelligence had finally been established. The Army data had their most immediate and profound impact on the great immigration debate, a major political issue at that time. Although the 1924 Restriction Act may have been passed without scientific support, the timing, and especially its peculiar character (i.e. imposing harsh quotas on nations of 'inferior stock'), clearly reflected the lobbying of eugenicists, using the Army data as their major weapon.

As we've seen, the Army tests had been constructed to measure innate intelligence; by definition, therefore, there was no room for the role of environmental influences.

As pure numbers, these data carried no inherent social message. They might have been used to promote equality of opportunity and to underscore the disadvantages imposed on so many Americans. Yerkes might have argued that an average mental age of 13 reflected the fact that relatively few recruits had the opportunity to finish or even to attend high school. He might have attributed the low average of some national groups to the fact that most recruits from these countries were recent immigrants who did not speak English and were unfamiliar with American culture. He might have recognized the link between low Negro scores and the history of slavery and racism. But scarcely a word do we read through 800 pages of any role for environmental influence.[51]

This quote seems to illustrate very clearly how dogma can determine the way that data are interpreted in order to produce scientific 'fact':

Once a theorist has formulated a view of something (in this case, the explanation of intellectual differences between national, ethnic and racial groups), all the data are moulded to fit the theory and, hence, apparently, to support it. The often claimed objectivity of science is sacrificed on the altar of a theory which the scientist must 'prove' at all costs.[52]

Yerkes, Terman and Goddard were already committed hereditarians before they came together to work on the Army tests. Three striking examples demonstrate the dogmatic nature of Yerkes's thinking:

1 He found a correlation of 0.75 between test score and years of education for 348 men who scored below average on Alpha: clearly, the less time spent in education, the lower the test score. Only ten had ever attended high school, four had graduated from high school, and only one had ever attended college. However, Yerkes argued that men with more innate intelligence spend more time in education: that's *why* they spend more time in education.
2 The strongest correlations of test score with schooling came from black–white differences. Once again, the fact that black people spend relatively little time in school compared with white people is explained in terms of a disinclination on the part of the former, based on low innate intelligence.

Yerkes seems to be mistakenly inferring a *cause* from a correlation: (a) it may be lack of schooling which causes the low test scores; and (b) there may be some third factor which accounts for *both* the low scores *and* the short period of schooling (such as racial segregation – at that time, officially sanctioned if not mandated – poor conditions in black schools and economic pressures to leave school and find work among the poor – which black people often are). You can only infer which of two correlated factors is the cause of the other based on some theory about how they're related;[53] in Yerkes's case, the hereditarian theory. He is presenting data to support a theory, but for that to work, the data must first be interpreted according to that very same theory – a classic example of *circular reasoning*.[54]

3 Half the black people from Southern states had not attended school beyond third grade (age nine), while half of those from Northern states had reached the fifth grade (age 11). Again, in the North, 25 per cent completed elementary (primary) school, compared with only 7 per cent from the South, and the percentage of Alphas was very much smaller and the percentage of Betas very much larger in the Southern than the Northern states. Why? Only the best Negroes had been smart enough to move North!

CULTURE AND INTELLIGENCE

All these black/white differences used to support the hereditarian theory are founded on the assumption that 'black' and 'white' denote distinct 'races'; the earlier discussion shows this to be an invalid assumption. The theory also makes another, equally invalid assumption, namely, that *culture* has no part to play in the measurement of intelligence. But *contextualization* is all-important:

> Rather than assuming that one would possess a certain 'intelligence' independent of the culture in which one happens to live, many scientists now see intelligence as an interaction between . . . certain . . . potentials and . . . the opportunities and constraints that characterize a particular cultural setting.[55]

This can be seen as an anti-hereditarian argument: Yerkes, Goddard, Terman and others *do* assume that intelligence can be measured separately from its cultural expression because it's essentially *biological*. While the action of biological evolution (Darwinian selection) is very slow, *cultural evolution* works quickly: differences between groups are likely to be more cultural than genetic in origin.[56]

According to the *cultural psychology perspective*, culture influences which behaviours are considered to be intelligent, the processes underlying intelligent behaviour and the direction of intellectual development. While not rejecting all use of psychometric tests, all measures of intelligence are culturally grounded, with performance dependent, at least partly, on culturally based understandings.[57] This would include the very experience of taking an IQ or any other type of psychometric test or taking part in any kind of academic research.

Psychological theories of intelligence must offer accounts that are *relative* to a particular time and context. But the hereditarians argue for a universal, culture-free, unchanging, objectively measurable, biologically determined property ('*g*' or 'general intelligence').[58] Furthermore, these 'universal' theories are associated with right-wing social philosophy, which their advocates aren't afraid of revealing. For example, in the preface to *The Bell Curve*,[59] the authors claim that 'Affirmative action [positive discrimination], in education and the workplace alike, is leaking poison into the American soul', and 'It is time for America once again to try living with inequality, as life is lived'. This kind of sentiment led *New York Times* columnist Bob Herbert to the conclusion that *The Bell Curve* 'is just a genteel way of calling somebody a nigger. The book has nothing to do with science'.[60]

PREJUDICE WITHIN PSYCHIATRY

Mirroring this last point regarding understanding the nature of intelligence:

> The appreciation and even the conceptualization of psychological difficulties can take place only within the set of available beliefs

and assumptions which are offered by one's cultural milieu – a set of assumptions which . . . involves the dominant as well as the minority culture, the doctor as well as the patient.[61]

While psychiatrists ('*alienists*') may judge certain behaviour on the part of patients ('*aliens*') as signs of an underlying (largely biologically-determined) mental disorder (or 'mental illness'), this may be a *meaningful* response to the situation from the patient's perspective.[62]

People judged to be mentally ill aren't the only 'aliens' or *outsiders*; they may also include all those groups that score low on both warmth and competence in terms of the stereotype content model (see Chapter 1), such as the poor and homeless. Other outsiders (who also score low on both warmth and competence) are immigrants, especially non-Europeans. While immigrants are initially 'outsiders from without', over time they may become 'outsiders in our midst', as are the mentally ill, poor, homeless and so on ('outsiders from within'). Homosexuals are aliens from within who, up until quite recently, have been regarded as mentally ill (see the next section).

Every society has its own distinctive pattern of behaviour and beliefs which, together, define 'normality'; if accepted patterns are seen as normal, we need a theory of *abnormality* or deviancy.

> However we conceive of our group, whether a class, a nation, or a race, we define it by those we *exclude* from it. These outsiders are perceived as different from ourselves. They may have different languages, different customs or beliefs. They may look different. We may even regard them as sick or as sub-human. However we define them we perceive them as an undifferentiated mass with no individual variations.[63]

Even if outsiders aren't physically dangerous, they always pose a threat to the *status quo* – because they're different.

> Their apartness is dangerous. It questions our tendency to see our society as the natural society and ourselves as the measure of

normality. . . . To confirm our own identity we push the outsiders even further away. By reducing their humanity we emphasize our own.[64]

THE SEXUAL ALIEN/OUTSIDER: HOMOSEXUALITY, MENTAL DISORDER AND THE LAW

The *Diagnostic and Statistical Manual of Mental Disorders* (DSM), published by the American Psychiatric Association (APA), is the 'bible' of American psychiatry and is also used throughout the world. In its second edition (DSM-II, 1968),[65] homosexuality was included as a *sexual deviation*, and, hence, was officially defined as a mental disorder.

In 1973, the APA Nomenclature Committee, under pressure from many professionals and gay activist groups, recommended that this classification should be removed and replaced with 'sexual orientation disturbance'; this was to be applied to homosexual men and women who are 'disturbed by, in conflict with, or wish to change their sexual orientation'. The change was approved, but not without fierce protests from several eminent psychiatrists who maintained the 'orthodox' view of homosexuality as inherently abnormal.

When DSM-III was published in 1980, another new term, *ego-dystonic homosexuality* (EDH), was used to refer to someone who is homosexually aroused, finds this arousal persistently distressing and wishes to 'become heterosexual'. DSM-III listed *predisposing factors* for all disorders, but not so for homosexuality, since this was no longer a mental disorder. As for EDH, two major predisposing factors were (i) the individual's internalization of society's *homophobia* (fear of homosexuals) and (ii) *heterosexism* (anti-homosexual prejudice and discrimination; see Chapter 1). So, according to the official classification of mental disorders, homosexual individuals are abnormal if they've been persuaded by society's prejudices that homosexuality is inherently abnormal – even though it denies that it is![66]

Not surprisingly, no such category as 'ego-dystonic heterosexuality' has ever been used.[67] When DSM-III was revised in 1987,[68] the APA decided to drop EDH (which was rarely used anyway). However, one of the many 'dustbin' categories, 'sexual disorder not otherwise specified', which included 'persistent and marked distress about one's sexual orientation', was retained in DSM-IV (1994),[69] DSM-IV-TR (2000)[70] and DSM-5 (2013). 'Ego-dystonic sexual-orientation' has also been dropped from the latest edition of the World Health Organization's (WHO) International Classification of Diseases (ICD-11, 2018–22).[71]

In the U.K. up until the 1960s, homosexuality among consenting adults was illegal; in 1995, the age of consent was lowered to 18.

> Clearly, nothing has happened to homosexuality itself during the last 30 years or so. What has changed are attitudes towards it, which became reflected in its official psychiatric and legal status. Homosexuality in *itself* is neither normal nor abnormal, desirable nor undesirable, and this argument can be extended to behaviour in general.[72]

THE ALIENIST/PSYCHIATRIST: OBJECTIVE SCIENTIST OR SCIENTIFIC RACIST?

As we have just seen when discussing changing classifications of homosexuality, norms change within the same culture over time. Hence, the criteria used by psychiatry to judge abnormality must be seen in a *moral context* – not a medical one. Psychiatry's claim to be an orthodox part of medical science rests upon the concept of mental illness ('*psychopathology*'), but far from being another medical specialty, psychiatry is a 'quasi-medical illusion'.[73]

Similarly, while the norms from which those with mental illness are believed to deviate have to be expressed in psychological, ethical and legal terms, the remedy (i.e. treatment) is sought in terms of *medical* measures. For this reason, the concept of mental illness can be seen as having replaced beliefs in demonology and witchcraft: it exists – or is 'real' – in exactly the same sense that witches existed or were 'real'.[74]

The concept of mental illness also serves the same *political* purposes. As we noted earlier, whenever people wish to exclude others (*aliens*) from their midst, they give them stigmatizing labels, such as 'mentally ill'.[75] Unlike those suffering from physical illness, most people considered to be mentally ill (especially those who are 'certified' or 'sectioned' and so *legally* mentally ill) are labelled in this way by *others* (including police and psychiatrists/*alienists*); they've upset the social order/*status quo* (by violating or ignoring social laws and conventions), and hospitalization represents a punishment for this 'crime'.[76]

The case of homosexuality's status as a sexual deviation demonstrates how 'mental illness' is a *social construction* rather than something which exists objectively in the way that physical disease exists: political forces determine the nature of what constitutes illness. Similarly, racist considerations are evident in the construction of two diagnostic categories reported in the U.S. at the time of slavery and described as peculiar to black people.[77]

- *Dysaesthesia Aethiopis* affected both mind and body, with 'insensibility' of the skin and 'hebetude' [dullness/lethargy] of mind, commoner among free slaves living in clusters by themselves than 'among slaves in our plantations and attacks only such slaves as live like free negroes in regard to diet, drinks, exercise etc.' Almost all 'free negroes' were afflicted by this condition 'if they had not got some white person to direct and take care of them'. So, the 'disease' was 'the natural offspring of negro liberty – the liberty to be idle, to wallow in filth, and to indulge in improper food and drinks'.

- *Drapetomania* is the 'disease causing slaves to run away'. After attributing the condition to 'treating them as equal' or frightening them by cruelty, Cartwright advocated a mixture of 'care, kindness, attention and humanity', with punishment 'if any one or more of them, at any time, are inclined to raise their heads to a level with their master or overseer . . . until they fall into that submissive state which was intended for them to occupy'.

The ridiculousness of *drapetomania* was pointed out by a contemporary of Cartwright:[78] not wanting/trying to run away would be a 'melancholy proof of imbecility or incipient dementia'.

The influence of ideological and political forces in determining diagnosis – and sometimes treatment – isn't usually as obvious as in these slave-related examples or in other multiracial settings such as apartheid in South Africa. In other cases, the importance of racial bias in the practice of psychiatry is often overlooked: in the U.S. and U.K., for example, racism in psychiatry isn't usually a matter of discrimination by individual practitioners or of an organized movement to deprive people of their rightful access to mental health services.[79] Rather:

> Racism within psychiatry derives from the traditions of the discipline, its history, its ways of assessing and diagnosing, the criteria it uses for designating treatment, its organization, its involvement with the powers of the state . . . and its struggle to be accepted as a scientific discipline.[80]

Similarly:

> Psychiatry reflects a system that is dictated by the broader prevalent social, political and economic structures. The availability of and access to health services remains dependent upon political and economic systems. Even when the members of minority ethnic groups seek help, they may well have to cope with individual and institutional racism.[81]

TAKING THE PATIENT'S HISTORY

This is often thought of as recording objective facts about the patient, but in reality, it's a highly *selective* account of whatever information has been obtained from the patient and others, and it's the psychiatrist who does the selection. The psychiatrist also influences the content of the history in two interrelated ways:

- The type and extent of information provided by the patient and others reflect how the psychiatrist perceives them. For example, if a black Asian patient says little about an arranged marriage (because he or she thinks the white psychiatrist will disapprove), this may well be interpreted by the psychiatrist as a negative quality (such as secretiveness or deviousness).
- The selection of information depends on the beliefs, value judgements, understanding and knowledge of the psychiatrist. White, middle-class psychiatrists are unlikely to have had personal experience of predominantly black areas (such as Harlem in New York, Tottenham in London or St. Paul's in Bristol), making them unaware of the pressures faced by their residents. This is likely to result in a misinterpretation of the patient's lifestyle and behaviour, which may well reinforce their (implicit) prejudices.[82]

ASSESSING THE PATIENT'S MENTAL STATE

This represents the other major feature of the *diagnostic interview* (along with history taking)[83] and is probably the major determinant of the final diagnosis. What the patient reports about his or her experiences is taken as evidence of an inner state of mind: it's taken quite literally as evidence that mental states exist in some objective way. However, the validity of such an inference is dubious at the best of times – even when there's excellent rapport and full understanding between the parties; in a multicultural/'multiracial' setting, it's highly unlikely that such rapport exists.

> The meanings attached to experiences and perceptions, the concept of illness, and the overall significance of the interview situation . . . are but some of the parameters along which variation must occur when cultural differences are present between the participants of an interaction.[84]

Deductions that are made from an 'examination' of the mental state *aren't* equivalent to a medical description of the state of a bodily organ, which has at least some degree of objective reality. 'What a doctor "finds" in a "mental state" is as much a reflection of the observer as of the so-called patient. It is a result of an *interaction* rather than a one-sided observation'.[85]

What this means is that the assessment and diagnosis that takes place within the context of psychiatry are fundamentally *social processes*, in which the prejudices, expectations, beliefs, values and personal experience of both patient and psychiatrist play a major role and which render the situation far less objective than it's often thought to be (especially by psychiatrists).[86]

An incredibly important feature of the social nature of psychiatric assessment is the *power imbalance* between psychiatrist and patient; this applies to the treatment situation as much as to assessment and diagnosis (see what follows).

> The ethnic-minority patients may not perceive the practice of psychiatry as benign. . . [it] is one way of legitimizing the suppression of non-normative behaviours that may threaten the society . . . mental health professionals may well represent the controlling nature of society, which may be perceived as oppressive. An ability to detain patients against their will and then treat them against their will gives a clear message to the community at large, and to members of ethnic communities in particular.[87]

Psychiatrists and therapists, by virtue of their position, training and experience, hold more power, and the therapeutic encounter (even if initiated by the patient) is dictated by the professional.[88]

The evidence suggests that non-white patients have good reason to regard the roles of psychiatrists and other mental health professionals as controlling and oppressive. Although less likely than the British-born to see a GP for psychiatric reasons, West Indian men are more likely to be admitted to psychiatric hospitals. Psychotic black patients are twice as likely as British-born and white immigrants to be involuntarily detained in hospital ('sectioned' under the Mental

Health Act). Asian-born patients in the U.K. are also more likely to be involuntary patients and less likely to refer themselves.

Black patients are more likely than white patients to see a black member of the psychiatric team and to see a junior rather than a senior doctor. Allowing for differences in diagnosis, black patients are also still more likely to be prescribed the most powerful antipsychotic drugs and to receive electro-convulsive therapy (ECT or 'shock therapy').[89]

SELF-DISCLOSURE AND PSYCHOTHERAPY

Members of minorities are less likely to have individual or group psychotherapy: they're seen as not meeting the 'ideal' criteria, one of which is the ability to *self-disclose*. Black clients, because of their past experience of racism and racial prejudice, often find it difficult to trust a white therapist and so find self-disclosure difficult.[90] For example, black clients will sometimes deliberately seek a black therapist because of their fear that to disclose certain family issues to a white therapist might produce a negative judgement of black people.[91] (This is directly equivalent to the earlier example of the Asian patient who fails to tell the white psychiatrist of the arranged marriage for fear of disapproval.)

Relationships with people in positions of authority are often influenced by one's racial heritage: a black client who is subservient in relation to the dominant white culture will relate to the therapist in basically the same way, seeing him or her as essentially 'in charge' of the encounter, expecting to be directed and instructed by the therapist. Some clients may even begin to doubt the therapist's competence if these expectations aren't met.[92]

Other black clients may be very anti-white, very angry with and distrustful of white professionals. But seeing a black therapist isn't necessarily the solution: such clients may see the black professional as 'selling out', adopting white majority, middle-class values and abandoning their own people ('white man in black clothing').

Alternatively, if they do decide to see a white therapist, they may look for ways to *sabotage* the relationship. What's certain is that there are very few black therapists.[93]

When a white patient/client meets a black psychiatrist/therapist, there's a *status contradiction* for the latter. The patient and his/her relatives have to reconcile their rather differing attitudes towards immigrants and doctors; they may become patronizing, feel they're getting second-class treatment and complain that a black doctor cannot understand them.[94]

So prejudice can work against both black clients and black professionals.

> Racism is neither a science nor a disease but a set of political beliefs which legitimates certain social and economic conditions. It is pointless to ask which is primary – prejudice or exploitation. They developed historically together, each validating the other.[95]

FEMINIST APPROACHES WITHIN PSYCHOTHERAPY

Some of the most radical feminist therapists are lesbian feminist therapists, and the more radical amongst these have been very critical of much of what takes place in the name of 'lesbian therapy' in particular and 'feminist therapy' in general.[96]

The central criticism is that the oppression of lesbians, in the form of homophobia and heterosexism, becomes 'transformed' into the psychopathology of individuals; i.e. since it is individual women who seek therapeutic help, the social and political roots of their problems are largely ignored, and therapy focuses on helping a woman to achieve higher self-esteem, better psychological adjustment and a more integrated self-identity. Although her psychological difficulties are often seen in terms of 'internalized homophobia' (the application to oneself of society's fear and hatred of homosexuals), the process of change is performed by individual therapists working with individual clients: *social* oppression, prejudice and discrimination become *individual* pathology.

However, the concept of 'feminist therapy' is a very fuzzy one: women therapists who support the general ideals of reformist feminism will often describe themselves as feminist therapists although they lack an integration of feminist theory into their work:

> Feminist therapy is not women therapists working with women on 'women's issues' (i.e. sexual abuse, body and eating) unless that practice is accompanied by explicit feminist analysis which ties individual distress to collective political struggles toward social change.[97]

At the same time:

> A feminist process of therapy respects the woman who walks in the door of the therapy office by meeting her at the point where she stands; rarely, in my experience, is this a place in which she is ready or willing to share her shamed inner self with a large community. Feminist therapy offers the lesbian client a safe base from which to make decisions about how to move her healing process into a broader sphere, while never losing sight of the relationship of the client and therapist both to that context.[98]

While Perkins and Kitzinger seem to regard all individual therapy for lesbians as 'selling out' to a homophobic, heterosexist, male-dominated society, Brown is arguing that individual therapy and political action (the latter, by definition, being a collective, 'community'-based process) are *complementary* and *equally necessary* aspects of change.

Agreeing with Brown, others argue that the ultimate question is: Does therapy work?

> If, through therapy, we improve our self-concepts and have more open, rewarding relationships with friends, lovers and children, who can say that it is a bad thing, a selling-out to mainstream culture?[99]

Similarly, instead of asking whether women should or shouldn't be doing therapy, we should be asking why the vast majority of those who are doing it are white and middle class: why do other 'race' and class groups see it as irrelevant or feel excluded from it?[100]

> Until the day that a feminist revolution has succeeded and there is no more violence against women and girl children, no more racism and sexism and hatred of lesbians and gay men, an end to anti-Semitism and the denial of access to people with disabilities – until that day when none of us faces the continuous reopening of these wounds and the physical and psychic danger inherent in living as a lesbian in patriarchy, there is a necessary and politically important function for feminist therapy practice with lesbians and other women and, clearly, for feminist means by which to engage in such practice.[101]

CONCLUSION

In Chapter 1 we defined prejudice and discrimination and looked at the different forms they can take and how they can change over time within the same sociocultural setting. While that discussion might seem to place prejudice and discrimination 'out there' in society, what I have tried to do in this chapter is to demonstrate that the scientific disciplines of biology, psychology and psychiatry, as part of wider society, aren't immune from these undesirable, but perhaps unavoidable, aspects of human nature. Indeed, the concept of 'race' that is so deeply-ingrained in human thinking – across cultures – originates from biology, which we wouldn't normally think of as embodying scientific racism. Similarly with psychology and psychiatry.

At first glance, the very concept of 'scientific racism' might seem nonsensical or, at least, inherently contradictory. Surely, we might think, the rules and procedures that are involved in science would guarantee – or at least enhance – objectivity, the very opposite of bias and prejudice. In the case of psychiatry, as a branch of medicine, surely its aim of helping people in psychological distress would be paramount, with issues of 'race', ethnicity, sexual orientation, social class etc. becoming largely irrelevant.

If this discussion has been 'successful', it would have shown these views of biological and psychological science and psychiatric practice (based on medical science) to be, sadly, rather naive. As we've seen, Darwin was 'inadvertently' racist, while some of the major pioneers of mental testing – Goddard, Terman and Yerkes – were blatantly racist even if they truly believed that their claims were based on 'objective facts'. While individual psychiatrists would probably reject the accusation of being racist, the institution in which they practice most definitely is.

As we've seen, we cannot separate these scientific disciplines from the wider sociocultural context in which they operate. In a racist society, it's normal – and inevitable – for major social institutions within it to display this racism, albeit in more subtle forms; it's also normal and inevitable that some individuals within those institutions will be racially prejudiced.

3

PREJUDICE AND PERSONALITY

PSYCHOLOGY AND PERSONALITY

In modern, Western experimental psychology, the study of personality represents a major source of *individual differences*, other major examples being age, gender and ethnicity. An example of personality differences that has seeped into our everyday understanding of human behaviour is the introversion–extroversion dimension,[1] according to which we can all be placed somewhere along this continuum; most of us will fall somewhere in the middle (we're neither extreme introverts nor extreme extroverts).

Research into introversion–extroversion and other major personality dimensions (such as neuroticism and psychoticism) has adopted a *psychometric* (mental measurement) approach: self-report questionnaires are used as an 'objective' measure of these various personality dimensions. As we saw in Chapter 2, one of the more controversial areas of psychological research –historically but also currently – is the measurement of differences in intelligence (IQ), particularly differences between different 'racial' groups. Intelligence testing, like personality research, adopts a psychometric approach, and intelligence, therefore, is another major way in which people (supposedly) differ from one another. The psychometric approach has played – and continues to play – a major role in the psychological study of prejudice.

A rather different approach to personality is adopted by psychologists such as Freud.[2] Again, some of his ideas have found their way into everyday understanding of human nature (such as 'ego', 'libido', 'repression'), but rather than being predominantly concerned with individual differences, he tried to describe and explain what people in *general* are like. For example, he believed that everyone passes through the same sequence of *psychosexual stages* from birth up to and including adolescence. However, people's *experiences* clearly differ, and this can help account for certain kinds of personality differences. As we shall see, Freud's theory plays a major role in the first major attempt by psychologists to explain prejudice.

STEREOTYPES, PREJUDICE AND PSYCHOLOGICAL ABNORMALITY

For much of the time that psychologists have been studying stereotypes and stereotyping, they've condemned them for being both false and illogical and dangerous; people who use them have been seen as prejudiced and even pathological.

Lippman[3] (who coined the term) described stereotypes as selective, self-fulfilling and ethnocentric, constituting a 'very partial and inadequate way of representing the world'. The early racial stereotyping research[4] was intended to trace the link between stereotypes and prejudice: stereotypes are public fictions arising from prejudicial influences 'with scarcely any factual basis'.

Although Allport argued that we can't help but think in categories (it's an inherent feature of human cognition: see Chapter 1), he also believed that prejudiced individuals tend to make extremely simple dichotomous judgements compared with tolerant, non-judgemental people ('faulty generalizations'). We also saw in Chapter 1 how Asch,[5] Sherif[6] and others argued that stereotypes need to be understood in the *intergroup context* in which they are used.

> To single out the most prejudiced, those who most accurately reflect the social view, and to call them mentally ill, is to find a scapegoat. We excuse ourselves by using the very mechanisms for

which we condemn the racist. Everybody who benefits by racism in a racist society is, in some measure, a racist.[7]

The quote above is referring to the *authoritarian personality*, which is discussed in what follows.

For many – both lay people and psychologists – blatant, overt, offensive racism is seen as the manifestation of a particular and probably pathological personality type. But even 'modern racism' is still portrayed by some researchers using the metaphor of an individual disorder (see Chapter 1): 'In modern racism, the overt symptoms have changed, but the underlying disease remains'.[8]

PSYCHOANALYTIC INTERPRETATION OF ANTI-BLACK PREJUDICE

According to some psychoanalytic theorists (based on Freud's theories), anti-black prejudice can be seen as a sequel to toilet training (which takes place during the 'anal phase' of psychosexual development), where the emphasis is on control, a balance between input and output, the development of a clear boundary between self and excrement (not self) and a preoccupation with dirt. Prejudice can be regarded as a projection of our own unacceptable desires onto scapegoats:

An accident of skin pigmentation allowed the European to use this early anal experience as a metaphor for later political realities: the black is equated with faeces, with the dirty part of ourselves. Clean/Dirty parallels White/Black, Us/Them.[9]

The 'anal personality type' identified very strongly with the parents, with rigidity and a denial of sensuality. He's the petit bourgeois, the frustrated little man who identifies with his superiors, denies his own wishes and projects them onto a group he considers beneath him. The roots of fascism were to be found in this type of personality configuration:[10] the unpleasant part of ourselves is located in other groups (for example, Jews and Asians crave power and influence, while the Irish and West Indians are bestial and stupid).

There are also associations with other body zones: fear of being swallowed up by blacks is commonly represented by cartoons of missionaries in cooking pots. As sensuality is denied in the white, the white woman is placed on an asexual pedestal out of the reach of the black penis.[11]

THE AUTHORITARIAN PERSONALITY

The best known and most influential (and one of the earliest) attempt to link 'collective ideologies' (such as fascism) to individual personality is presented in Adorno et al.'s *The Authoritarian Personality*.[12] It uniquely blended Marxist social philosophy, a Freudian account of family dynamics and quantitative psychometric attitude research. It quickly established itself as reference point for a whole generation of researchers into the causes of prejudice.[13] According to Billig, the theory 'constitutes a major landmark in the history of psychology, as well as being the single most important contribution to the psychology of fascism'.[14]

Adorno et al. began by studying anti-Semitism in Nazi Germany in the 1940s. After their emigration to the U.S., they embarked on studies with more than 2,000 college students and other native-born, white, non-Jewish, middle-class Americans (including schoolteachers, nurses, prison inmates and psychiatric patients). Their research combined large-scale psychometric testing and individual clinical interviews, all designed to test the basic hypothesis that an individual's political and social attitudes cohere together and are 'an expression of deep lying trends in personality'.[15] Prejudiced people are susceptible to racist/fascist ideas prevalent in their society at a given time.

THE F-SCALE

The psychometric work was initially concerned with designing some objective measures of various forms of overt prejudice, namely *anti-Semitism* (the AS scale), *ethnocentrism* (E scale) and *political and economic conservatism* (PEC scale). These then evolved into the construction of a personality inventory which would tap the central aspects of the underlying authoritarian personality syndrome (the F-scale or *potentiality for fascism*), intended to measure 'pre-fascist tendencies';[16] this comprised 38 items, including questions concerned with:

- *conventionalism* ('Obedience and respect for authority are the most important virtues children should learn')
- *authoritarian submission* ('Young people sometimes get rebellious ideas, but as they grow up they ought to get over them and settle down')
- *authoritarian aggression* ('Sex crimes, such as rape and attacks on children, deserve more than mere imprisonment; such criminals ought to be publicly whipped or worse')
- *power and toughness* ('People can be divided into two distinct classes: the weak and the strong')
- *projectivity* ('Nowadays, when so many different kinds of people move around and mix together so much, a person has to protect himself especially carefully against catching an infection or disease from them')
- *sex* ('Homosexuals are hardly better than criminals and ought to be severely punished')

The scale correlated well with their previous measures of intergroup prejudice, despite containing no items specifically referring to ethnic groups.

To validate the F-scale (i.e. to show that it actually measured what it claimed to measure, namely, potentiality for fascism), small sub-samples of very high or very low scorers on it were selected for intensive clinical interviews, comprising detailed questioning regarding recollection of early childhood experiences, perception of parents and views on various current social and moral issues. These seemed to confirm many of their theoretical suppositions about the origins and consequences of authoritarianism for example:

1 High scorers tended to idealize their parents as complete paragons of virtue.
2 High scorers remembered their childhood as a time of strict obedience to parental authority with harsh sanctions for misdemeanours.

Their current attitudes corresponded well to their answers on the F-scale: they were very moralistic, openly condemnatory of 'deviants' or social 'inferiors', displayed sharply defined categorical stereotypes and were often openly prejudiced. By contrast, low scorers painted a more equivocal and balanced picture of their early family life and typically presented a more complex and flexible set of social attitudes.

HOW DOES THE AUTHORITARIAN PERSONALITY BECOME PREJUDICED?

Based on the interview data, which included the use of *projective* tests (whereby participants are asked to say what they see in ambiguous images, such as ink blots, revealing *unconscious* thoughts and feelings), Adorno et al. claimed that authoritarians have often experienced a harsh, punitive, disciplinarian upbringing with little affection. While they consciously held their parents in high esteem, they often revealed *latent* (unconscious) hostility towards them, stemming from the extreme frustration they experienced as children.

Drawing on Freudian theory, Adorno et al. proposed that such unconscious hostility may be *displaced* onto minority groups who become *scapegoats*. Authoritarians also *project* their own unacceptable, antisocial (especially sexual and aggressive) impulses onto these groups, making them objects of fear. They have very little insight (self-understanding), and their prejudice serves a vital *ego-defensive function*: it protects them from the unacceptable parts of themselves.

SUPPORTIVE EVIDENCE FOR THE AUTHORITARIAN PERSONALITY THEORY

One early approach was to test the association between authoritarianism and mental rigidity. For example, as predicted, those who scored high on ethnocentrism showed consistently more mental rigidity (on simple arithmetical problems) than low scorers.[17]

Following several failed attempts to replicate this finding, it was concluded that this connection only emerged when the testing situation was important for participants (socially, scientifically or personally *ego-involving*).[18]

An alternative approach was to measure *perceptual ambiguity*. Using the autokinetic effect (a visual illusion in which a stationary spot of light in a dark room appears to move), it was found that ethnocentric participants were less tolerant of perceptual ambiguity than non-ethnocentric ones.[19] When participants estimate how far the light 'moves' on a number of different occasions, their estimates eventually stabilize: for those high on ethnocentrism, this happened much faster than those low on ethnocentrism (indicating greater *intolerance* of ambiguity).

So there's at least some early evidence that more authoritarian (or prejudiced) people do tend to think in a particular way. But what of the link between authoritarianism and prejudice?

Adorno et al. found significant correlations (usually greater than 0.6) between their earlier measure of outright ethnocentrism and the F-scale, thus confirming their hypothesized link between prejudice and personality. Subsequent studies have replicated this finding. For example, one study found a similar-sized correlation in a sample of U.S. students between authoritarianism and their own measure of xenophobia which tapped hostility towards blacks, Jews, Mexicans, Japanese and English.[20]

A cross-national comparison also found reliable correlations (0.4–0.6) between F-scale and anti-black prejudice.[21] A study in the Netherlands reported consistent and substantial correlations between (i) authoritarianism and ethnocentrism and (ii) authoritarianism, sexism and support for extreme right-wing political groups.[22] An Indian study found that religious prejudice against Muslims, caste prejudice against Harijans and sexist prejudice were all predictable from the authoritarianism of some high-caste Hindu men. The three measures of prejudice correlated highly with each other, further supporting the idea of an underlying prejudiced personality.[23]

Also consistent with Adorno et al.'s theory are observed correlations between authoritarianism and attitudes towards stigmatized or deviant subgroups. For example, studies have found that authoritarians were less sympathetic than non-authoritarians towards mentally ill people even when the respondents were actually staff in psychiatric institutions.[24] Similarly, attitudes towards people with AIDS may be less positive among authoritarians.[25] Authoritarianism in men has been found to correlate with both sexual aggression towards women and guilt associated with past sexual aggression.[26]

IS THERE ANY EVIDENCE THAT CHALLENGES THE AUTHORITARIAN PERSONALITY THEORY?

Despite this range of supportive evidence, some of the reported correlations weren't very strong, usually explaining less than half and sometimes less than a fifth of the variance in prejudice scores. So whatever the contribution of personality disposition to expressed prejudice, there are clearly other processes at work.[27]

Occasionally, zero correlations have been reported between authoritarianism and outgroup rejection. For example, among English-speaking respondents in Canada, there was a significant correlation – as predicted – between authoritarianism and anti-French feeling, although this was very weak (< 0.2). However, the same group showed a *negative* correlation between authoritarianism and a measure of nationalism (the higher the one, the lower the other) and no correlation at all with internationalism. Even more difficult to explain were the consistent null relationships amongst the francophones.[28]

A study of *xenophiliacs* – people who are *attracted* towards strangers/foreigners (the opposite of xenophobia) – found that they tended to be *more* authoritarian than their less xenophilic peers – the *opposite* of what Adorno et al. would have predicted.[29]

Their account is *reductionist*, that is, explaining a *social* phenomenon (racism) in terms of characteristics of *individuals* (racial prejudice; see Chapter 1). Adorno et al. believed this was a problem for sociological or political analysis. But this not only distracts attention away from institutional racism, it also fails to answer the key questions of why particular minority groups in particular historical periods become the scapegoats.[30] It also fails to provide any understanding of the kind of racism that locally passes for common sense and that seems to require no personal 'pathology' (as in apartheid).[31] The claim that we inevitably 'think in categories' also adds to this individualizing of racism: it becomes both an inherent feature of the human mind and 'normal'.

METHODOLOGICAL CRITICISMS OF THE F-SCALE

Adorno et al.'s sample was rather unrepresentative; despite its size (more than 2,000 in the test of the F-scale alone), participants were drawn mainly from formal (and predominantly middle-class) organizations.

As with all their scales, all the F-scale items were worded such that agreement with them indicated an authoritarian response: any authoritarianism so measured cannot easily be distinguished from a general tendency to agree with seemingly authoritative-sounding statements[32] (this is called the acquiescence/positive response set). Although acquiescence may be indicative of authoritarianism, it more likely reflects the ambiguous nature of many items.[33]

The steps taken to validate the F-scale through in-depth clinical interviews left much to be desired; in particular, the interviewers knew in advance each respondent's score, which could have influenced the answers they elicited.[34]

Adorno et al. found correlations between authoritarianism and intelligence, level of education and social class; these were found to be even stronger in later research.[35] This suggests that authoritarianism might simply reflect the socialized attitudes of particular subgroups in society and doesn't derive from a certain kind of family upbringing.[36]

The F-scale was unable to predict authoritarian behaviour: it appeared to be nothing more than a measure of authoritarian attitudes, which helps to explain the frequently observed significant relationships between F-scale scores and various measures of prejudiced attitudes.[37]

THE DOGMATIC PERSONALITY: LEFT-WING AUTHORITARIANISM

As Adorno et al. measured and described it, authoritarianism represents only one variant, namely, right-wing. Based on historical and political sources, it has been argued that people with other political views can also be authoritarian.[38] Rokeach[39] developed and generalized this argument into a more systematic psychological theory.

Rokeach distinguished between (i) the *content* of a prejudiced person's beliefs – the specific set of intolerant attitudes re: the outgroup targets; and (ii) how these beliefs are *structured*. Could left-wingers be equally authoritarian, albeit targeting different outgroups, as in the virulent rejection of Trotskyists and other so-called 'revisionists' by Stalinists?[40] What these apparently very different kinds of prejudice have in common is a similar underlying cognitive structure in which different belief systems are well isolated from one another, resistant to change in the light of new information. This describes the 'closed mind' or *dogmatic personality* (as opposed to the open-minded/ non-prejudiced person).

To substantiate his theory, Rokeach devised the Dogmatism Scale, which aimed to tap general authoritarianism. Although some items were very similar to the F-scale items and shared the latter's positive response set, he hoped that his scale would be a more content-free index of authoritarianism.

Rokeach tried to demonstrate its *validity* in various ways. In two small studies, he compared the dogmatism scores of groups of students judged by their professors or peers to be especially dogmatic or very open-minded. The groups didn't differ significantly on measured dogmatism when professors' judgements were used as criterion, but the scale was more discriminating when peer ratings were used.

In further studies, Rokeach compared the dogmatism scores of groups which he intuitively considered to be more dogmatic than average (e.g. avowed Catholics, members of left-/right-wing political groups) with those he considered less dogmatic (e.g. non-believers, political liberals). He also used Adorno et al.'s measures of authoritarianism and ethnocentrism. There was some support for his claim that dogmatism was a more general measure than authoritarianism. For example, a rather small group of communists scored the same as conservatives on dogmatism but considerably lower on authoritarianism. These same communists scored marginally higher than Liberals on dogmatism but lower than them on authoritarianism, suggesting that it might be possible to distinguish general intolerance from a right-wing political position in a way that the F-scale seemed not to do.

Rokeach, like Adorno et al., believed that the dogmatic ('closed-mind') personality stems from early family socialization, especially relationships with parents. He expected that dogmatic people would display the same exaggerated glorification of their parents and symptoms of repressed anxiety (e.g. nightmares, nail-biting). Consistent with this, he found[41] that open-minded students were more likely to describe their parents in equivocal/ambivalent terms and to recollect fewer symptoms of childhood anxiety. But it was the 'intermediate' rather than the extremely closed-minded group who showed the greatest contrast with this group.

HOW USEFUL IS 'DOGMATISM' FOR PREDICTING PREJUDICE?

The amount of research is very limited compared with the authoritarianism research. One study found that dogmatism correlated with whites' anti-black attitudes in the U.S. (even after controlling for education, socio-economic status/SES and geographical location).[42] In another, dogmatism correlated with anti-Arab prejudice – although not strongly – among fundamentalist religious groups in Israel.[43]

AUTHORITARIANISM AND TOUGH-MINDEDNESS

Eysenck[44] also argued that people's disposition towards intolerance was independent of their left or right leanings; he called this *tough-mindedness*, which he claimed is associated with *extroversion*. Such people are more resistant to social conditioning by family/other social influences and so would be more likely to endorse/adopt extreme (i.e. unconventional) social and political attitudes; these would probably be tinged with strong elements of punitiveness or aggression (since these tendencies, too, would be less restrained than in more 'normally' socialized individuals).

However, very conservative (and prejudiced) attitudes weren't always found to be positively correlated with *extroversion* (for example, one researcher found a significant *negative* correlation.[45] So Eysenck subsequently proposed that *psychoticism* and not *extroversion* is the main personality dimension underlying tough-mindedness.[46] Some researchers claimed that people's social attitudes – including their levels of prejudice – might be genetically determined.[47]

Apart from the rather unconvincing empirical evidence for both Rokeach and Eysenck, perhaps the most damning criticism of attempts to equate extremism of different political persuasions has been made by Billig.[48] He argues that the measuring instruments used in this research area are far from being politically neutral (and thus able to detect purely psychological distinctions); indeed, they actually contain items that are ideologically biased. So any observed differences or similarities between groups are attributable to the aggregation of political attitudes elicited by the particular mix of items on any given scale. For example, members of the Communist and National Front parties in the U.K. *could* be clearly distinguished by a careful analysis of the individual items they endorsed on Rokeach's[49] Value Survey instrument.[50]

RIGHT-WING AUTHORITARIANISM

The authoritarian personality explanation lost favour and lay dormant for many years. It was re-branded as *right-wing authoritarianism* (RWA), which comprises authoritarian *submission* (obeying powerful leaders), *authoritarian aggression* (inflicting harm on those who deviate from conventional beliefs, especially when harming is sanctioned by one's leaders) and *conventionalism* (conforming to traditional values).[51] To be classified as an RWA, one has to manage all three. Using the RWA scale, distinct from the original F-scale, significant correlations between RWA scores and prejudice, punitiveness and tolerance of government injustices against unconventional victims were reported. Such individuals tend to be members of right-wing political parties, but, surprisingly, they'd support government action aimed at severely restricting the activities of both fringe left-wing and right-wing groups.[52]

While generating only limited research, RWA is seen as breathing new life into an old idea; it consistently correlates with prejudice against a variety of outgroups.[53]

SOCIAL DOMINANCE ORIENTATION (SDO)

SDO refers to the degree to which one endorses a hierarchy in which some groups dominate other groups.[54] People high on SDO support policies that maintain inequality (e.g. opposing affirmative action/positive discrimination[55]) and choose careers that *enhance* existing hierarchies (such as business, police work, public prosecution) rather than teaching, social work or public defence (which *attenuate* existing hierarchies). Thus, SDO is a crucial motivator that underpins ethnic and group inequalities. All human collectivities lead to the formation of social hierarchies, which are group based with one hegemonic group at the top (e.g. whites in the U.S.).

Men are more likely than women to be high on SDO and are correlated with being tough-minded and seeing the world as a competitive place.[56] High SDO favours the powerful. For high-status groups, high SDO exaggerates ingroup favouritism. Even for low-status groups, if they view the hierarchy as legitimate, high SDO also predicts favouring the high-status group.[57]

One way to understand the relationship between various individual differences and prejudice is in terms of the kind of threat posed to the ingroup:[58]

- *Authoritarianism* focuses on perceived threat to *ingroup values* in a dangerous world.
- *SDO* focuses on perceived threat to *ingroup status* in a competitive world.

This constitutes the *dual-process theory of ideology and prejudice*: this identifies two separate paths to ingroup favouritism/outgroup prejudice:[59]

- punitive socialization → social conformity → viewing the world as dangerous → RWA → ingroup favouritism/outgroup prejudice
- unaffectionate socialization → tough-mindedness → viewing the world as competitive → SDO → ingroup favouritism/outgroup prejudice.

There's strong research support for the links between socialization, personality, world view and ideology in U.S., Europe, South Africa and New Zealand.[60]

SDO has been found to correlate significantly with political-economic conservatism, nationalism, patriotism, cultural elitism, anti-black racism, male gender, rape myths and sexist attitudes towards women. People high on SDO were also unlikely to support a range of policy initiatives, including women's rights, gay and lesbian rights and racial equality.[61] But they were quite likely to endorse law-and-order policies, military programmes and chauvinism.

PREJUDICE AND BELIEF IN A JUST WORLD

According to the *just world hypothesis* (JWH), we tend to view the world as essentially a fair and just place where people get what they deserve and deserve what they get.[62] When 'bad' things happen to people, we believe it's because they're in some way bad, so they've at least partly 'brought it on themselves'. This can help explain 'blaming the victim'. For example, in rape cases, the woman is often accused of having 'led the man on' or giving him the 'sexual green light' before changing her mind.[63]

A German civilian, on being shown round the Bergen-Belsen concentration camp following the British liberation in 1945, commented, 'What terrible criminals those prisoners must have been to receive such treatment'. S/he refused to be believe (or couldn't) that such horrors (as had obviously been perpetrated in the camp) could have happened to innocent people – if these things happened to them, why couldn't they happen to me?[64]

Believing in a just world gives us a sense of being in control: so long as we're 'good', only 'good' things will happen to us. Without a sense of control, the world would seem to be arbitrary, with people at the mercy of uncontrollable forces.[65] High scorers on just world measures tend to blame the poor for their plight,[66] show very little sympathy for those with HIV/AIDS,[67] are less sympathetic to feminist ideology[68] and derogate those on Social Security benefits.[69]

> Thus, the tendency to 'blame the victim' is a self-serving attribution and functions to protect individuals from others' misfortune. By blaming the victim, we are able to rationalise societal inequalities by attributing the failings of individuals to their own dispositions, rather than to some weakness of social institutions.[70]

An Australian study found that just-world beliefs predict negative attitudes to those with HIV/AIDS in men but not in women. This might reflect differences in traditional gender socialization: females are raised to be caring and supportive, while males are encouraged towards mastery, self-reliance and aggressiveness. Men, therefore, see these people as deviant, incompetent and undeserving of sympathy.[71]

CONCLUSIONS: LIMITATIONS OF A PERSONALITY APPROACH TO PREJUDICE

While there may be individuals with racist and/or other prejudiced attitudes (e.g. the authoritarian personality), this cannot account for why a society *as a whole* may be racist. Racist attitudes may manifest as a highly articulated set of beliefs in the individual, but they're also found in less conscious presuppositions, located in society as a whole.

The personality approach underestimates – or even, in its strongest form, completely ignores – the power and importance of the immediate social situation in shaping people's attitudes – including intergroup relations. One of social psychology's rare 'true' field (naturalistic) experiments demonstrated the *lability* (changeability) of prejudice.[72] Two groups of American female students were observed over a 12-month period: one group had been *randomly* allocated to a very conservative/traditional sorority housing, the other to much more liberal housing. The latter showed a marked decline in their authoritarianism; the former hardly changed at all. The measure used was the F-scale, supposedly an index of a temporally and situationally *stable* personality feature!

Similarly, the study of black and white coalminers in West Virginia demonstrated the *situational specificity* of prejudice:[73] below ground there was almost complete integration, but complete segregation above! Also, there's a large research literature showing how *intergroup contact* can reduce outgroup hostility (see Chapter 6).

Unsurprisingly, white South Africans and Southern whites in the U.S. showed high levels of anti-black prejudice. At the individual level, this was correlated with authoritarianism, but the overall sample means (averages) for authoritarianism were no higher than in other less-prejudiced groups, i.e. in terms of their overall distribution of personality types, they were rather similar to 'normal' populations despite their overtly racist attitudes.[74] As in Minard's study of coalminers, it was the social norms they were exposed to that outweighed any personality dysfunction.

Several other studies have examined the origins of prejudice in South Africa: socio-demographic variables have been consistently good predictors of levels of prejudice, independently of levels of authoritarianism. For example, Afrikaans speakers and lower-SES groups have tended to be more prejudiced than English-speaking or middle-class groups.[75]

A major difficulty for any personality account is explaining two interrelated phenomena:

1 the *uniformity* of prejudiced attitudes across whole social groups, as in Nazi Germany and apartheid South Africa; and
2 the *historical specificity* of prejudice: the sudden rises and falls of prejudice over time, as in Nazi Germany again, and also

anti-Japanese feeling in the U.S. before and after Pearl Harbour, 1942; the latter – at both a personal and institutional level, including the establishment of large prison camps for Asiatic Americans – took place over just months.[76]

These and other historical changes suggest that authoritarianism may actually be an effect of changing social conditions rather than deriving from particular child–parent relations. The observed correlation between authoritarianism and prejudice, rather than indicating a causal relationship between them, may actually stem from their joint dependence on a third factor, namely these wider societal factors (changing social conditions).

If personality factors are important at all, then it's probable that they are so for those at the two extremes of the distribution of prejudice: the perpetually tolerant and the unremitting bigot. For the remaining large majority, personality may be a much less important determinant of prejudice than the many and varied *situational* influences on behaviour. Furthermore, for these people it may even be more appropriate to regard personality as itself an effect of those same social and cultural variables rather than as a causal agent in its own right.[77]

4

THE IMPACT OF ENVIRONMENTAL FACTORS ON PREJUDICE AND DISCRIMINATION

WHAT DO WE MEAN BY 'ENVIRONMENTAL'?

When evaluating the personality approach in Chapter 3, we had cause to contrast individual personality (be it authoritarianism, dogmatism, tough-mindedness, right-wing authoritarianism or social dominance orientation) with factors *beyond* or *acting on* the individual (such as conforming to social norms and intergroup relations) to shape his or her prejudices.

We noted that even if we accepted the 'reality' of the authoritarian personality (as measured by, say, the F-scale), that in itself couldn't account for specific cases of widespread anti-outgroup prejudice and discrimination, as in anti-Semitism in Nazi Germany and the anti-Japanese response to Pearl Harbour. Clearly, there were particular historical, social, economic and political events and forces that converged to create those situations; these events and forces can probably also explain authoritarianism, anti-Semitism etc. as measured by Adorno et al.,[1] better than a particularly prevalent kind of child-rearing can explain them.

These events and forces are what we mean by 'environmental' factors in this context. For younger generations growing up in Germany in the 1930s, some of these events and forces may have seemed quite remote, such as Germany's defeat in World War I; for those who lived through that war, they may have been very real. The aftermath of that defeat was something that affected all Germans: while most didn't join the Nazi party, millions submitted to Hitler's regime.

FEAR OF FREEDOM: *THE VIEWS OF ERICH FROMM*

Fromm, like Freud, was a psychoanalytic theorist (and therapist), but one major area of disagreement between them concerned the influence of social, cultural and historical forces on human behaviour.

In The Fear of Freedom,[2] Fromm argued that human beings are both part of nature and apart, separate from it. We created primitive creeds and religious beliefs to enable us to feel less separated from the world, and in Europe, until very recently, the Catholic Church fulfilled this role of providing a sense of security; it mediated between God and humanity, guaranteeing salvation but, in the process, limiting human freedom.

The Reformation and the rise of Protestantism broke the power of the Catholic Church, giving people their freedom – but at what price?

> Separation – both physical and psychological separation from nature, and psychological separation from dogma and authority – makes people free. But separation makes people alone, and potentially insignificant and lonely.[3]

At least while Protestantism thrived and remained influential, people still had a meaningful place in the universe. But with the rise in the 19th century of industrialization, capitalism and science, the universe was turned into a machine, with no room for God; this left people alone and insecure and their lives without meaning.

One solution to this existential problem is to create and become part of authoritarian organizations and totalitarian regimes, such as those of Hitler's Germany and Stalin's Russia. People like Hitler and Stalin surrendered their freedom by continuously making 'bad' choices; eventually, they could only choose what was wrong. While their behaviour was, ultimately, determined, earlier in their lives they were able to make choices. But freedom is never absolute and always depends on what alternatives are available.

We all face a fundamental decision: either we accept, even welcome, our freedom, or we can choose to escape from it (our 'ultimate' acts of freedom, perhaps) by surrendering ourselves and our freedom to a person, ideology or organization.

THE FRUSTRATION-AGGRESSION HYPOTHESIS

Another limitation of the personality approach that we noted in Chapter 3 is that outgroups, the targets of hostile feelings and discriminatory behaviour, aren't selected arbitrarily or randomly. If personality, such as a low threshold of tolerance of being frustrated, were all there was to prejudice and discrimination, then this is exactly what they'd be.

The *frustration-aggression hypothesis* (FAH),[4] originally an attempt to explain aggression, has been used to explain discrimination. However, while personality is a major source of individual differences (see Chapter 3), the FAH was more concerned with the universal human tendency to react in certain predictable ways to frustration.

According to the FAH, frustration always – and inevitably – produces aggression, and conversely, aggression is always – and only – caused by frustration. The source of frustration – defined as whatever prevents us from achieving our goals – might sometimes be a fairly powerful and visible threat (such as parents or our boss), while at other times it may be difficult to identify (such as 'people with money', 'foreigners' or 'the government').

Drawing on Freud's psychoanalytic theory, the FAH claims that when we need to vent our frustration but are unable to do so directly, we *displace* it onto a substitute target: we vent it *indirectly* through finding a *scapegoat* (usually a weaker person or group, less able to retaliate or make us pay for our aggression). Historical examples also suggest that majority group norms make displaced aggression towards particular scapegoats more acceptable than if other scapegoats were targeted. The choice of scapegoat is far from random.

In the U.K. during the 1930s and 1940s, it was predominantly Jewish people who were scapegoated, who were replaced by African-Caribbean people during the 1950s and 1960s, followed by Asians from Pakistan, India, Bangladesh and East Africa during the 1970s, 1980s and 1990s. Despite widespread migration to the U.K. from Poland, Hungary and the Ukraine after World War II, these groups weren't targeted in the same way – at least not until the 2016 EU Referendum. Also, there has been a sharp increase in anti-Muslim prejudice and discrimination in both the U.K. and U.S. coinciding with an increase in terrorist attacks by Islamist groups. Simultaneously, far-right groups in Europe and the U.S. have perpetrated more anti-Semitic terrorist acts.

In the southern states of the U.S., lynchings of black people between 1880 and 1930 were related to the price of cotton: as the price dropped, the number of lynchings increased.[5] While this is consistent with the concept of displaced aggression, the fact that white people chose black people as scapegoats rather than some other minority group suggests that there are usually socially approved (or *legitimized*) targets for frustration-induced aggression.

RELATIVE DEPRIVATION THEORY

According to the FAH, people experience frustration when they feel deprived of something which they believe is in their grasp – and which they're entitled to. The discrepancy between our *actual* attainments (such as standard of living) and what we *expect* to attain (the standard of living we feel we deserve) is our *relative deprivation* (RD).[6]

When attainments suddenly fall short of rising expectations, RD is particularly acute; this often results in collective unrest. This is well illustrated by the 1992 Los Angeles riots. The immediate trigger was the acquittal, by an all-white jury, of four LA police officers accused of beating a black motorist, Rodney King. Against a background of rising unemployment and continuing disadvantage, the acquittal was seen by the black community as symbolic of their low esteem in the eyes of the white majority.[7] The great sense of injustice produced by the acquittal seemed to demonstrate in acute form the injustice which is an inherent feature of discrimination – and of RD. The Black Lives Matter movement, starting in the U.S. in 2013, demonstrates that this (sense of) injustice is as strong as ever.

The LA riots also illustrate *fraternalistic* RD, based on a comparison either with other individuals who are *different* from oneself or with other groups.[8] In contrast, *egoistic* RD is based on comparison with other *similar* individuals. White people who expressed the most anti-black prejudice were those who felt most strongly that whites, as a group, were badly off relative to blacks. Objectively, they were actually *better off*, illustrating the *subjective* nature of RD.[9] Similarly, riots in Minneapolis in May 2020 were triggered by the blatant murder of George Floyd, an African American, by a white police officer.

REALISTIC GROUP CONFLICT THEORY (RGCT)

According to RGCT, intergroup conflict arises as a result of a conflict of interests: when two groups wish to achieve the same goal but only one can do so, hostility between them is produced.[10] Indeed, conflict of interest (or *competition*) is a *sufficient* condition for the outbreak of hostility or conflict. This claim is based largely on the Robbers Cave experiment,[11] which has been described as the most successful field experiment ever conducted on intergroup conflict.[12]

THE ROBBERS CAVE EXPERIMENT

This was actually the third of three summer camp experiments (1949, 1953 and 1954) conducted in three different locations. The setting for the last of these (reported in 1961) was Robbers Cave State Park in Oklahoma, where 22 white, middle-class, Protestant, well-adjusted boys spent two weeks at a summer camp. They were randomly assigned to two groups of 11, each occupying a separate cabin, out of sight of the other. All the boys were strangers prior to their arrival at the camp.

During the *first stage* of the experiment, each group co-operated on a number of activities (pitching tents, preparing food, a treasure hunt), and soon a distinct set of norms, rules and standards emerged which defined the group's identity. One group called itself 'the Rat-tlers' and the other 'the Eagles', each with its own flag, anthem, dress code, leaders and followers. Towards the end of the first week, the two groups were informed of the other group's existence, and an 'us' and 'them' language quickly developed.

The *second stage* began with the announcement that there was to be a 'grand tournament' between the two groups, comprising ten sporting events, plus points awarded for the state of their cabins and so on. A 'splendid trophy' would be awarded to the winning group, plus medals and four-bladed knives for each member of the winning group.

Throughout the tournament, the adult camp leaders (the research team) deliberately fanned rivalry between the Rattlers and Eagles, cov-ertly stacking the odds against one team then the other; this increased the tension and kept the scores neck and neck. Hostilities reached fever pitch halfway through. The Rattlers' faces were smeared with soot as they crept up to the Eagles' cabin in darkness; days of warring and fights followed, with staff only intervening to break things up before there was a serious injury.[13]

AN EVALUATION OF THE RGCT

The Robbers Cave experiment was designed to demonstrate the belief that people are inherently good; it is the economic, political and social environment that sets groups competing against each other, breeding rivalry and prejudice. However, as we've seen, the rivalry and hostility between the Rattlers and the Eagles was at least partly manipulated by the researchers; this hardly counts as objective, independent evi-dence for the RGCT. (The theory reflected Sherif's political beliefs as a Turkish immigrant to the U.S. at the time of the Great Depression. He had to temper his anti-capitalist views when reporting the study, as this was the time of the McCarthy anti-communist 'witch hunt'.)[14]

The GCT is arguably the most obvious explanation for how preju-dice and discrimination arise.[15] However, it has received only limited and inconsistent support, and the perceived, symbolic threat posed by outgroups is more important than any real or tangible threat (see discussion of the *Intergroup Threat Theory* in the next section). For this reason, the 'realistic' may as well be dropped from its name, and the theory renamed 'perceived group conflict theory'.[16]

An attempt to replicate the Robbers Cave study produced very different findings.[17] English Boy Scouts at their annual camp, who knew each other well prior to the start of the camp, engaged in very similar activities to those of the Rattlers and Eagles. They were divided into four 'patrols', competing in situations familiar to them from previous camps, but the friendship ties which predated arrival at the camp were maintained across the four patrol groups. Competition remained friendly, and there was no increase of ingroup solidarity: the leader deliberately encouraged the four groups to continue to see themselves as part of the larger, inclusive scout group.

Sherif et al.'s findings reflect the transitory nature of their experimental groups. The fact that the English boys knew each other beforehand, had established friendships, were familiar with camp life and had a leader who encouraged co-operation were all important *contextual/situational* influences on the boys' behaviour.[18]

> It seems, then, that 'competition' may not be a sufficient condition for intergroup conflict and hostility after all. If we accept this conclusion, the question arises whether it's even necessary; in other words, can hostility arise in the *absence* of conflicting interests?[19]

(Attempts to answer this question are discussed in Chapter 5.)

THE INFLUENCE OF THE MEDIA

Media routinely highlight minority group membership in relation to negative events, such as crime and social problems; they can be thought of as an influential source of *indirect contact* (see Chapter 6), as they communicate intergroup events to minority and majority audiences on a daily basis. For example, in Flemish-Belgian newspapers, immigrant minorities are commonly represented as threatening the welfare, culture and safety of the majority group. Similarly, Dutch newspapers most often associate ethnic minorities with negative issues such as crime and less often with positive or neutral issues such as culture, employment and education.[20] (In the U.K., both historically – at least since the 1950s – and still, immigrants are portrayed by the tabloids as 'stealing' the jobs that are the right of people born in this country.) As media messages involving minority group members are negatively biased, media constitute a chronic source of intergroup threat.

According to *Intergroup Threat Theory* (ITT),[21] when particular outgroups are perceived as a source of threat to the ingroup, people will develop negative psychological and behavioural reactions towards this threatening group. Accordingly, negative attitudes towards devalued outgroups (such as immigrant, ethnic or religious minorities) are often informed by threatening media messages concerning crime, violence or other social problems involving outgroup members. ITT incorporates both RGCT (see earlier) and *social identity theory* (SIT),[22] according to which people are motivated to achieve and protect a positive social identity: negative attitudes will arise from perceived threat at a *symbolic* level of ingroup values or identity.

An example of the role of media in intergroup threat is the Amsterdam street murder (in 2004) of Theo Van Gogh, a controversial Dutch journalist and filmmaker, who was accused of blasphemy and stabbed to death by a Moroccan-Dutch Muslim. The murder attracted considerable national and international media attention and added to the strain on the already tenuous intercultural relations between majority and Muslim minority populations in the Netherlands. Importantly, Dutch media presented differing views of the murder and its repercussions on both sides of the Dutch–Muslim divide; the predominant view of a clash between Muslim and Dutch values was challenged by two main alternatives: an extremist act and a violation of religious values.[23]

One group of researchers wished to investigate when it is that people go along with threatening media messages, generalizing the wrongful acts of a single individual to the outgroup as a whole, and when they resist such threat. What makes some people less susceptible to threat in the media?[24] Drawing on intergroup contact research (see Chapter 6), these researchers proposed that the *perceived typicality* of an outgroup actor is a crucial moderator of generalized attitudes.[25] If a perpetrator is seen as a typical outgroup member, his (or her) offensive act is defined as *normative outgroup behaviour*; this makes it much more likely that threat perceptions and negative evaluations will generalize to the whole outgroup ('they're all the same'). As we shall see in Chapter 6, most empirical support for the role of perceived typicality has been found in studies of *positive* intergroup contact. What effect will typicality have in the context of negative situations such as the Van Gogh murder?

This research also explored how perceived typicality can be situationally influenced by presenting other outgroup members who approve or disapprove of an outgroup perpetrator's behaviour. It was predicted that when disapproving outgroup members portray the perpetrator as a deviant (or anti-normative) member, perceived typicality will be reduced; by contrast, outgroup approval will enhance perceived typicality and hence the generalization of negative feelings to the outgroup as a whole. In turn, disapproving outgroup members will help reduce intergroup threat. In three separate but linked studies involving Dutch majority participants and undergraduate students, support was found for all of these predictions.[26]

TERRORISM AND THE INTERNET

While far-right and white supremacist extremists represent a tiny minority of the majority groups in the U.S., Europe and other wealthy, developed countries, their most hated outgroups include minority groups, in particular Jews and Muslims. In turn, most terrorist acts aimed at the white majority in those countries in the last 20 years have been committed by Islamist extremists, acting either as part of a terrorist cell or as loners.

It's widely agreed that terrorism is evil, but there's little agreement as to why it has increased so much in the 21st century.[27] However, it's clear that *globalization* has played a crucial role:

> 21st-century globalization is, in important ways, new and central to the macro, collective processes shaping terrorism. . . [these] and not the personality of individuals are the major factor leading to the rise of terrorism.[28]

In turn, 'contemporary globalization is driven primarily by powerful technological and economic factors'.[29] Central to the technological side of this equation is the Internet.

The 'Magnificent Seven'[30] refer to factors which collectively explain the Internet's power to create a unique psychological space, namely:

1 Feeling of anonymity
2 Control over level of physical exposure
3 High control over communication (between ourselves and our social contacts and the content of messages we'd like to make known)
4 Ease of locating like-minded people
5 Accessibility and availability at all times and places
6 Feeling of equality
7 Fun of web surfing

Regarding anonymity and control over physical exposure, perpetrators believe that no one will be able to identify them no matter what they do, and so they'll go unpunished; at the same time, the victim is unlikely to have any countermeasures available. Perpetrators may operate initially within a non-violent community or may exist as an organized community of aggressors who seek out particular victim groups (based on 'race', sexual orientation, religion etc.). Even if a violent site is removed (such as a 'race'-hate group), the perpetrators can always find another server somewhere in the world where they can upload the same offensive content.[31]

Perpetrators' high degree of control over their communications makes them feel empowered, while the victim feels helpless and vulnerable. This sense of control derives partly from the *remote* nature of their aggression (not face to face); this, combined with their anonymity, removes inhibitions against aggression, which may become increasingly extreme.[32] Victims may be *dehumanized* (see Chapter 1). Increasingly extreme behaviour may also occur as a means of strengthening the sense of belonging to the online ingroup.

Frustrated, marginalized individuals can find themselves metaphorically rubbing shoulders with others whom they'd never approach in the real world. Chatrooms and forums are 'completely hate-centred environments wrapped in fun, interactive ribbons; for example, a Nazi-friendly site (www.americannaziparty.com) offers computer games whose goal is to kill as many Jews as possible'.[33]

DOES THE INTERNET MAKE GOOD PEOPLE BAD?

Rather than changing people in some fundamental way, the Internet can be seen as providing a virtual environment which helps free people from the usual social restraints; this can sometimes result in the unleashing of previously suppressed violent tendencies. It allows aggressors to ignore social norms and escape their usual identities ('discard the mask'):

> In that sense, it seems that the Internet has created paradise on earth for violent people. In this paradise, there are any number of ways to express violent tendencies: paedophilia, invasion of privacy, information theft, racial and religious incitement, intellectual property violation, and terrorism.[34]

So, while Internet-channelled violence can take many forms, racial and religious incitement, which is often terrorism related, is the most relevant to our discussion of the causes of prejudice and discrimination. Just as Allport[35] identified five forms of discrimination, increasing in the potential harm they can produce for the victims (see Chapter 1), so it's possible to identify a corresponding list of Internet-related forms of discrimination: the planning of terrorist acts – and their subsequent execution – would sit at the top of this most heinous hierarchy.

CONCLUSIONS: DO THE MEDIA ONLY PRODUCE NEGATIVE EFFECTS?

Long before the advent of the Internet and social media, psychologists were investigating the effects of film, television, comics, then video (especially 'video nasties') and violent video games.[36] The focus was very much on the effects of media *violence* on children and early adolescents: Did exposure to such media content make young viewers more likely to become aggressive or violent themselves?[37]

To properly evaluate the media violence research, we must first consider the moderating role of individual differences (see Chapter 3) and cultural and contextual factors (as discussed earlier and in Chapter 5). What this implies is that media violence – and all other content – only has an *indirect* effect on viewers' behaviour. For example, how TV violence is *perceived* and *interpreted* are clearly important *intervening variables*. Again, *desensitization* refers to the reduction in emotional response (and related physiological arousal) to violent content – and an increased acceptance of violence in everyday life – as a consequence of repeatedly viewing it.

One meta-analysis ('study of studies') involved 280 separate investigations – up to the year 2000 – of the effects of violent content in TV movies, video games, comic books and music,[38] concluding that the evidence for a link is almost as strong as that between smoking and lung cancer and even stronger than that between condom use and HIV prevention. More recent meta-analytic reviews have supported these conclusions: there is a *causal* link between media violence and aggressive or violent behaviour. While both short- and long-term effects may be small, they *accumulate* over time to produce significant behavioural changes.[39]

Some psychologists draw different conclusions, claiming, for instance, that media violence is neither necessary nor sufficient; aggressive behaviour is multiply determined, and media violence can be a contributing factor to some aggressive acts in some individuals.[40] However, despite these and other dissenting voices, the overwhelming weight of evidence seems to point in the direction of a causal link between media violence and aggressive behaviour.

However, if TV can produce *antisocial* behaviour such as aggression and discrimination, then, presumably, it can also have *positive* effects, promoting *prosocial* behaviour. Indeed, there's an emerging research literature suggesting that prosocial media that portray helping behaviours can have equally strong positive effects, reducing antisocial outcomes and increasing prosocial ones.[41]

5

THE INFLUENCE OF GROUP MEMBERSHIP

As we saw in Chapter 4, the *realistic group conflict theory* (RGCT)[1] claims that objective competition between groups is a *sufficient condition* for prejudice and discrimination to arise. The theory was based on the famous Robbers Cave field experiment,[2] which created 'real ethnocentrism, real stereotypes, and real perceived injustice' by assigning previously unacquainted strangers to groups, allowing them to establish a group identity, and then putting these groups into competition with each other.[3]

However, even assuming that it is sufficient (and the study of English Boy Scouts that we described in Chapter 4 challenges this conclusion[4]), we still need to ask if it is actually *necessary*. In other words, can prejudice and discrimination occur (or be created) in situations in which there is *no* competition? Another way of asking this question is: Does the fact of belonging to one nationality, religion, ethnic group or social class in *and of itself* generate predictable orientations towards members of other nationalities etc.?[5] If so, what is the 'minimal case' for producing them?

MINIMAL GROUPS

The *mere perception* of another group's existence can produce discrimination.[6] When people are arbitrarily and randomly divided into two groups, knowing that the other group exists is a sufficient condition for the development of pro-ingroup and anti-outgroup attitudes. These artificial groups are known as *minimal groups*.

Before any discrimination can occur, people must be categorized as members of an ingroup or an outgroup (making categorization a *necessary* condition). More importantly, the very act of categorization produces conflict and discrimination (making it also a *sufficient* condition). These conclusions are based on the creation of artificial groups among 14- and 15-year-old Bristol schoolboys. The criteria used to create the groups were arbitrary and superficial and varied between experiments. They included: (i) chronic 'overestimators' or 'underestimators' of the number of dots appearing on slide projections; (ii) preference for paintings by Klee or Kandinsky; and (iii) the toss of a coin. Whatever the boys believed to be the basis for being assigned to one group or another, the actual assignments were always random.

Once these minimal groups had been formed, each boy worked alone in a cubicle on a task that required various matrices to be studied (two rows of numbers one on top of the other, the top row representing the points that could be awarded to the boy's own group and the bottom row the points that could be awarded to the outgroup). Each boy had to decide how to allocate the points to a member of his own group (but not himself) and an outgroup member; they were also told that the points could be converted to money at the end.

All each boy knew about another boy was whether he belonged to the same group or the other group; otherwise, he was anonymous, unknown, unseen and identified only by a code number.

So what did the boys do?

When they had a choice between *maximizing* the profit for everyone (*maximum joint profit*/MJP) and *maximizing* the profit for ingroup members, they acted in the interest of the ingroup. With a choice between profit for everyone *and* for their own group – as opposed to the ingroup winning *more* than the outgroup at the expense of both these utilitarian advantages – it was the maximization of *difference* that seemed more important.

Similarly, *ingroup choices* (between two members of the ingroup) were consistently and significantly nearer to the MJP than were the *outgroup choices* (between two members of the outgroup). *Fairness* was also an important influence: most choices were compromises between fairness and ingroup favouritism.

EVALUATION OF THE MINIMAL GROUP EXPERIMENTS

These have been described as some of the most influential and provocative studies in the entire study of intergroup processes.[7]

Other experiments have gone even further than those of Tajfel et al. by actually *telling* participants they were being randomly assigned, tossing a coin in front of them or giving them obviously meaningless names (such as As and Bs or Kappas and Phis).[8] Even under these conditions, the groups still showed a strong ingroup preference.

Intergroup discrimination in this minimal group experimental setup (or *paradigm*; MGP) has proved to be a remarkably robust phenomenon. In more than two dozen independent studies, experimental participants of varying ages, essentially the same result has been found: the mere act of allocating people to arbitrary social categories is sufficient to elicit biased judgements and discriminatory behaviours.[9] One interesting exception to this rule involved white and Polynesian children in New Zealand;[10] the latter showed themselves to be much more generous towards the outgroup, reflecting cultural norms which emphasized co-operation.

The MGP has been criticized on several methodological and theoretical grounds, especially its artificiality and meaninglessness.[11] But it's precisely the need to find meaning in an 'otherwise empty situation' (especially for the self) that leads participants to act in terms of the minimal categories ('Klee'/'Kandinsky' etc.);[12] in fact, you can turn the meaningless argument on its head:

> The power of minimal categorizations to produce group-based behaviour reflects the customary significance and usefulness of categorical perception which participants import to the laboratory – when a context is defined in social categorical terms *participants expect the categories to mean something*.[13]

SOCIAL IDENTITY THEORY (SIT)

Although outgroup discrimination is very easy to trigger, unlike the Robbers Cave experiment, neither an objective conflict of interests nor hostility had any relevance whatsoever to what these Bristol schoolboys were asked to do. It was enough that they saw themselves as clearly categorized into an ingroup and an outgroup – despite the arbitrary/random nature of the categorization. This was true despite the fact that they knew each other well beforehand, there were no individual gains at stake, and their choices could have been aimed at achieving the greatest common good.

The boys' choices were influenced by two major social norms: 'groupness' and 'fairness'. They managed to achieve a neat balance between the two in this experimental situation, but in real life, socialization into 'groupness' is powerful and unavoidable.[14]

In order to simplify and bring order to our 'social construction of reality', we gradually learn to classify social groups as 'we' and 'they', or 'us' and 'them' (ingroups and outgroups, respectively). This combines with the hostility inherent in many of the group stereotypes we're constantly exposed to and produces 'generic norms' of behaviour towards outgroups (discriminating against them in favour of the ingroup).[15] This is a process that's both more general and goes deeper than either the learning of value judgements about a specific group or conformity. It has three consequences:

1 There may be discrimination against an outgroup even if there's no reason for it in terms of the individual's own interests (what s/he can gain from any such discrimination).
2 Such discrimination may occur in the absence of any previously existing hostility or dislike towards the outgroup.
3 This generic norm may manifest itself directly in behaviour towards the outgroup *before* any prejudice or hostility has developed.

The conclusion that's usually drawn from the Robbers Cave experiment is that prejudice and hostility between the two groups were a *consequence* of the competition between them manipulated by the researchers. But the first response to hearing of the other group's *existence* was to express a wish to challenge them. This intergroup rivalry occurred *before* the actual competition had been announced: just being in one group and becoming aware of the other seemed to trigger feelings of competitiveness. The minimal group paradigm is an attempt to create experimental conditions that would enable us to assess the effects of *intergroup categorization* as such – uncontaminated by other variables.[16]

'Groupness' and intergroup categorization lie at the heart of *social identity theory* (SIT).[17] Despite the methodological and other criticisms made of the MGP, the findings from minimal group experiments formed the basis for SIT, a major attempt to explain intergroup discrimination, ethnocentrism and hostility.

Dividing the world into a manageable number of categories not only helps us to simplify and make sense of it (as do stereotypes: see Chapter 1) but also serves to help us define who we are. Our *sense of identity* is closely bound up with our various group memberships.[18] We all strive to achieve or maintain a positive self-image, which has two components: *personal identity* (the personal characteristics and attributes which make each person unique) and *social identity* (a sense of who we are, derived from the groups we belong to). In fact, we each have several social identities corresponding to the different groups we identify with (ingroups); in each case, the more positive the image of the ingroup, the more positive our own social identity and hence our self-concept (in particular, our *self-esteem*). By emphasizing the desirability of the ingroup(s) and focusing on those distinctions which enable our ingroup(s) to come out on top, we help create for ourselves a satisfactory social identity.

Some individuals may be more prone to prejudice because their personal and social identities are much more interconnected than for those with a lesser need for social acceptance. Prejudice can be seen as an *adjustive mechanism* which bolsters the self-concept of those who feel personally inadequate – but with potentially undesirable social implications. (Some supportive evidence comes from the study of white supremacists in the U.S.)

HOW CAN SIT ACCOUNT FOR THE MINIMAL GROUP EXPERIMENTS?

As we've noted, SIT emerged from the findings of the minimal group experiments and was an attempt to account for those findings. The use of code numbers for group members produces a feeling of anonymity in a meaningless group; the only possible source of identity is in the ingroup – primitive as it is – and the only way to make it distinguishable in a positive way from the outgroup is to allocate more points to ingroup members. However, if we have to favour the ingroup in order to distinguish it from the outgroup, isn't this the reverse of what happens under 'normal' circumstances? Groups which we have already identified as 'in' or 'out' (they're already distinguished) are favoured (or not) because they're 'in' or 'out'?[19]

This relates to the very 'status' of the MGP. The arbitrary/artificial nature of minimal groups is so far removed from our real-life group memberships that we might ask if they have any ecological (real-world) validity at all. In turn, how valid can SIT be if it's derived from the minimal group findings?[20]

AN OVERALL EVALUATION OF SIT

SIT has been criticized on the grounds that it presents racism – and other forms of prejudice – as 'natural', helping to justify it. Stemming from Allport's claims that stereotypes are 'categories about people' and that we can't help but think in categories,[21] Tajfel saw the process of categorization as a basic, inherent feature of human thought.[22] From this, racism (understood as a form of intergroup hostility or ingroup favouritism) may also be construed as natural. In terms of the distribution of resources, racism is thereby justified as the norm ('charity begins at home').[23] Of course, Tajfel never intended SIT to be seen as justifying racism – he was a Jew and lost his family and community in the Holocaust.

Also, to further bolster defence of SIT in the light of these accusations and to contextualize it, it's quite fitting that the study of minimal groups and the subsequent SIT should have occurred in Europe (rather than, say, in North America). European history is littered with accounts of intergroup conflict, and, as noted, Tajfel was a Jewish survivor of Hitler's 'Final Solution'.

While there's plenty of evidence of intergroup discrimination, this appears to stem from the evaluation of the ingroup (a *positive ingroup bias*), as distinct from derogatory attitudes or behaviour towards the outgroup (a *negative outgroup bias*, which is what we usually understand by 'prejudice': see Chapter 1).[24] Indeed, SIT suggests that prejudice consists largely of liking 'us' more than disliking 'them'; favouring the ingroup is the *core* phenomenon.[25]

Similarly, whether or not differentiation results in negative treatment of the outgroup depends on what's valued within the ingroup's belief system. Indeed, SIT challenges the notion that people in groups are inherently inclined to act oppressively towards others and thereby challenges the view that there are fundamental biases in collective thinking.[26]

However, recent evidence suggests that the mere act of categorizing ourselves as belonging to an ingroup (and so, by definition, defining others as belonging to an outgroup) is sufficient for us to see *less humanity* in the latter's faces.[27] Participants were shown images from a computer-generated series in which the face of a Barbie doll morphs incrementally into a human face. If the face was designated as one of their own group (a fellow student at their university), participants perceived it as looking human *sooner* than if they believed it was the face of someone from a different university; i.e. the *threshold* for perceiving an ingroup member was *lower* (less stringent). ('Being human' was defined as having a mind, so the more human the image *looked*, the sooner it was *attributed* with a mind.). The researchers believe that our social identity powerfully affects how we evaluate others, including how much humanness we accord them; these evaluations occur perhaps within the first half second of seeing someone.[28]

Despite these problems, SIT (and *self-categorization theory*, an extension of it[29]) has been a major influence on European (especially British) social psychology.[30] Regardless of the debate over the validity of minimal group experiments and SIT in explaining intergroup conflict, SIT is one of the few theories to propose a 'thoroughly social understanding of the person and to regard the social realm as more than a set of variables which may come to influence the ready-made person'.[31]

What Burr means by this is that 'the person' can only be understood as a social being, and part of what that entails is being perceived by others – and perceiving oneself – as belonging to certain social groups and not to others. The ingroup/outgroup differentiation is a major part of what makes us who we are. By the same token, racism only arises within a particular social context, where 'racial' categories become significant and acquire meaning as group divisions. These categories aren't natural but become powerful as a result of social history.[32] (See Chapter 2.)

CONCLUSIONS: CULTURE AS PART OF HUMAN NATURE, CO-OPERATION AND FAIR INEQUALITY

We rely more than any other species on the accumulated knowledge of our ancestors to survive and prosper: for the most part, we embrace our culture because it's our ticket to the future. Our disposition for culture evolved because it led to the greatest reproductive success. We seem programmed willingly to accept the culture of our birth: 'it is hard to adjust to a new cultural environment once the one we were born into has been installed into our minds'[33] – as evidenced by the resistance to stamping out culturally defined emotions, such as xenophobia and racism.

However, in liberal democracies there's immense concern about all kinds of inequality ('inequality aversion') – both in these countries and in other, non-democratic societies. The focus is, typically, on prejudice and discrimination relating to gender, sexual orientation, religion and ethnic background; this perhaps reflects the wired-in tendency towards unequal treatment of different groups within most cultures, both historically and culturally. But we cannot defend prejudice and discrimination on the grounds that it's part of human nature and the fight for gender, sexual, religious and racial equality is *morally straightforward*.[34]

However, the battle against *economic* inequality is rather more complicated. When people are surveyed about the ideal distribution of wealth, they actually show a preference for *unequal* societies: they aren't bothered about inequality *per se* but rather about *economic unfairness*. Human beings naturally favour *fair* distributions of wealth – not equal ones. When fairness and equality clash, people generally prefer *fair inequality* over *unfair equality*. So, for example, it's fair that someone with an exceptional talent or who works much harder than most people should earn more than the rest of us; conversely, it would be unfair if everyone was paid the same regardless of the hours they work, the skills or training required to do the job etc.[35]

This intuition for fairness seems to be deeply ingrained ('wired in'): it's what allows humans to work together in large groups. Wouldn't you prefer to work with someone who puts in at least a fair share of the effort and takes at most a fair share of the reward to someone who's lazy (a 'free-rider') or greedy? Likewise, other people will prefer to work or interact with you if you have a reputation for fairness:

> Over our evolutionary history, individuals who cooperated fairly outcompeted those who didn't, and so evolution produced our modern, moral brains, with their focus on fairness.[36]

6

REDUCING PREJUDICE AND DISCRIMINATION

In Chapter 3, we considered explanations of prejudice in terms of individual personality. What this approach implies for reducing prejudice is that, somehow, we need to change what people are like or prevent them from developing certain types of personality.

In the case of the authoritarian personality, parents could, in theory, be trained/educated to use child-rearing methods that would prevent the child from experiencing excessive frustration or repressed anger towards them which later in life gets displaced onto minority or other outgroups; this takes the form of prejudiced feelings and cognitions and discriminatory behaviour. However, even if it could be shown that particular patterns of child-rearing have a particular and direct effect on the child, we'd still face insurmountable difficulties – both practical and ethical – regarding the implementation of alternative, 'safer' methods. There's always the possibility that there are *several* routes to developing an authoritarian personality, with child-rearing that combines control with little affection being just one of these.

The impact of environmental factors discussed in Chapter 4, namely, conformity to social norms, relative deprivation, and competition between groups for scarce/limited resources, are, arguably, more intuitively appealing as explanations of prejudice and discrimination – as well as helping to distinguish between them. But again, as with the authoritarian personality example, the logical conclusion to be drawn from this explanation is that in order to reduce the impact of social norms etc., those norms would themselves have to be changed.

As we saw in Chapter 1, stereotyped beliefs – the cognitive component of prejudice – reflect an apparently in-built, inherent aspect of human thinking: we cannot help thinking in categories, a form of generalization in which large numbers of individuals are grouped together as members of a particular category. This alone suggests that some degree and kinds of prejudice are inevitable, although the affective/feeling components are more influential (see Chapter 1). We also noted that discrimination can and does occur in the absence of either stereotyped beliefs or strong negative feelings: the drive to conform, and, hence, feel accepted by others and that one belongs, is very powerful and is sometimes a sufficient reason for discriminatory behaviour.

Changing norms is a lengthy and challenging process, and those norms which relate to prejudice and discrimination often involve some of the most fundamental values and beliefs about what's 'good', 'normal' and 'desirable'.

Similarly, if relative deprivation and competing for scarce resources are 'real' social processes that can sometimes validly account for prejudice and discrimination, it's because they reflect the way that most societies – in both the West and the East, both developed and developing, rich and poor – are structured. Inequality, be it between male and female, white and black, working class and middle/upper class etc., is an inherent feature of large human populations. Prejudice and discrimination are symptomatic of those divisions, and changing those divisions is almost synonymous with human history itself.

The focus of Chapter 5 was on the influence of group membership and group identity. Whether we're talking about ingroups or outgroups, membership or reference groups, majorities or minorities, minimal/random groups or real-life groups, they represent a fundamental feature of both social structure and individual self-concept/identity. Directly or indirectly, it is the focus on inter-group relations that has provided the theoretical – and practical – basis for social psychological research into reducing prejudice and discrimination.

THE CONTACT HYPOTHESIS

Probably the first formal proposal of a set of social-psychological principles for reducing prejudice was Allport's *contact hypothesis* (CH, as it's come to be known; see Chapter 1).[1] Almost 70 years after its original formulation, the CH remains one of the dominant theoretical and applied frameworks for reducing prejudice and improving intergroup relations.

According to the CH, positive contact between groups is the key, provided that four conditions are met: (i) *equal-status contact* between the groups in the pursuit of (ii) *common* (or *superordinate*) *goals*, conducted in a (iii) *co-operative* (as opposed to competitive) *spirit* ('common humanity') and (iv) *sanctioned by institutional supports* (by law, custom or local atmosphere).

The original CH claimed that all four conditions are necessary – and together are sufficient – for the reduction of prejudice and discrimination. Until quite recently, most of the research aimed at testing the CH has focused on the first two conditions: equal-status contact and common superordinate (goals).

EQUAL-STATUS CONTACT

WHY IS THIS IMPORTANT?

As we noted in Chapter 1, Allport gave five examples of 'discrimination', including *avoidance* (which, more formally, can take the form of *segregation*). When people are segregated, they're likely to experience *autistic hostility*, that is, ignorance of others, resulting in a failure to understand why they behave as they do. Lack of contact means there's no 'reality testing' against which to check our interpretations of others' behaviour; in turn, this is likely to reinforce negative stereotypes (see Chapter 1). In the same way, ignorance of 'what makes them tick' will probably make 'them' seem more *dissimilar* from ourselves than they actually (objectively?) are. Bringing people into contact with each other should make them seem more familiar and, at least, offers the possibility that this negative cycle can be interrupted and even reversed.[2]

Related to autistic hostility is the *mirror-image phenomenon*:[3] groups in conflict come to see themselves as being in the right (with 'God on their side') and the enemy in the wrong. Both sides tend to attribute to each other the same negative characteristics ('the assumed dissimilarity of beliefs'). Increased contact provides the opportunity to disconfirm our stereotypes, the outgroup becomes less strange, and group members are more likely to be seen as unique individuals, rather than an 'undifferentiated mass' (the *illusion of outgroup homogeneity/outgroup homogeneity effect*:[4] While we tend to stereotype the outgroup ('they're all the same'), we tend to see all kinds of individual differences among members of our own groups (the *ingroup differentiation hypothesis*[5]).

HOW EFFECTIVE IS EQUAL-STATUS CONTACT?

It's generally agreed that increased contact in and of itself *won't* reduce prejudice. Although we seem to prefer people who are familiar, if this contact is between people of consistently unequal status, then 'familiarity may breed contempt'.[6] Many white people (in the U.S.) have always had considerable contact with African Americans – as dishwashers, toilet attendants, shoe-shiners, domestic servants etc.[7] – but such contacts may simply reinforce white people's stereotypes of African Americans as socially and intellectually inferior. Similarly, we need to ask under what conditions does intergroup contact have an impact, for whom and regarding what outcomes?[8]

One early study of equal-status contact compared two kinds of housing project in the U.S. One was thoroughly integrated (black and white people were assigned houses regardless of race), while in the other the two groups were segregated.[9] Both casual and neighbourly contact was greater in the integrated project, with a corresponding reduction in anti-black prejudice among whites.

As we noted in Chapter 4, many cases of segregation and other forms of discrimination can be explained in terms of conformity to social norms. Norms that dictate behaviour in different situations can dramatically influence relations between the same groups in those different situations. This was starkly illustrated by Minard's study of coalminers in West Virginia: there were two distinct (contradictory?) sets of norms, one that required equal status when the men were working in the mines (for the sake of safety and efficiency) and another that required segregation in their non-working lives (in line with mainstream and widespread anti-black prejudice and discrimination).

Similarly, research has shown that interracial attitudes improved markedly when black people and white people served together as soldiers in battle and on ships – but relationships weren't so good at base camp.[10]

In a review of a number of studies of desegregation in U.S. schools, it was concluded that white anti-black prejudice wasn't reduced, while black anti-white prejudice seemed to have *increased*.[11] However, very few of these studies involved a school situation in which all four of Allport's conditions were in place at the same time.[12]

A much-cited meta-analysis ('study of studies') involving 515 studies (all relevant studies conducted to that date), 250,000 participants in 38 nations, found an *inverse relationship* between intergroup contact and prejudice: the *greater* the intergroup contact, the *lower* the prejudice.[13] The size of this inverse effect (or *negative correlation*) is comparable to (i) the inverse relationship between condom use and sexually transmitted HIV and (ii) the *positive correlation* between passive smoking and incidence of lung cancer at work.[14] This meta-analysis also showed that contact effects hold equally well for groups other than the races and ethnicities at whom the CH was originally aimed. We should note that fully 71 per cent of these studies had been conducted in North America.

PURSUIT OF COMMON (SUPERORDINATE) GOALS

In a co-operative situation, the attainment of one person's goal enhances the chances of other group members attaining theirs; this is the reverse of a competitive situation.[15]

A much-cited demonstration of this co-operation comes in the final part of the classic Robbers Cave field experiment described in Chapter 4.[16] Following the violence between the Rattlers and the Eagles that occurred as a result of the tournament, the researchers arranged that the camp's drinking water supply was cut off and the only way to restore it was by a co-operative effort. Also, in order to afford the cost of hiring a movie, both groups had to chip in, and, finally, when the truck got stuck on a trip to Cedar Lake, the boys had to pull together on a rope to get it free.

In the final few days of the camp, the group divisions disappeared, and the boys actually suggested travelling home together in one bus. Sixty-five per cent of their friendship choices were now made from the other group, and their stereotypes became much more favourable.

One influential attempt to create both mutual cooperation and equal-status contact is the *jigsaw classroom*.[17] This is a learning technique first used in schools in Austin, Texas, in 1971 shortly after the city schools had been desegregated and children from different ethnic backgrounds were taught together in the same classrooms for the first time. Tension had built up between the groups during the first few weeks, resulting in actual fights; a school superintendent ('head teacher') called in the psychologists to help remedy the situation. After observing mixed classes for a few days, they concluded that the hostility between the different ethnic groups was fuelled by a competitive atmosphere; what was needed was to transform this competitive climate into a co-operative one.

The resulting jigsaw classroom is a highly structured method of *interdependent learning*, in which children are assigned to six-person inter-racial learning groups. The day's lesson is divided into six distinct parts, and each group member is assigned material which represents one piece of the lesson (the 'jigsaw') to be learned. Each child must learn its part and then communicate it to the rest of the group; at the end of the lesson, the children are tested on the whole lesson, and each is given an individual score. So each child is dependent on the other five group members for parts of the lesson that can only be learned from them. Hence, there's complete mutual interdependence.

The aim of the research programme which produced and evaluated the jigsaw classroom method was to develop a classroom atmosphere that could be sustained by the classroom teacher long after the psychologists had left. Every pupil/student spends some time in the role of expert, and the most important, unique feature of this method is that each has a special, vital gift that's unavailable elsewhere.[18]

The jigsaw method has been used now for almost 50 years, and its effectiveness has been demonstrated in several studies in which children are randomly assigned to either a jigsaw classroom or a traditional classroom. These studies have consistently shown that those taught in jigsaw classrooms not only come to like each other more but also perform better in exams and have higher self-esteem than those taught in traditional classrooms.[19] But do they become less prejudiced? Does this increased liking for the particular children in their classroom groups extend to how they feel about these other ethnic groups *as a whole* (i.e. do the effects of the jigsaw classroom *generalize*)? The evidence here is inconclusive: while the method makes some intergroup perceptions more positive, this doesn't usually amount to a wholesale liking for different racial groups as a whole. This may be partly accounted for by the fact that many studies are small-scale and relatively short-term interventions. Also, the method works best with young children before prejudiced attitudes can become deeply ingrained.[20]

However, there's now much greater optimism that positive effects can generalize in several ways: across situations, from specific outgroup members to the whole outgroup, from the immediate outgroup to other outgroups (the *secondary transfer effect*[21]) and across different types of responses.[22] For example, one study found that contact across the Catholic–Protestant sectarian divide in Northern Ireland promoted not only more positive attitudes towards the religious outgroup but also towards racial minorities.[23]

DO SUPERORDINATE GOALS ALWAYS HELP REDUCE PREJUDICE?

If the co-operation fails to achieve the superordinate goal, anti-outgroup feeling may actually *increase*. Groups need to play distinctive and complementary roles, whereby each group's contribution is clearly defined; when this doesn't happen, liking for the other group may *decrease*, perhaps because group members are concerned with the ingroup's integrity.[24]

In the case of successful co-operation, the generalization of positive feelings from particular outgroup members to the outgroup as a whole will only happen if group boundaries are maintained (*mutual differentiation*[25]). For example, contact with grandparents was a much better predictor of more positive attitudes towards 'the elderly' in general when young people reported being aware of age groups during contact.[26]

However, isn't it possible that emphasizing group/category boundaries during contact will reinforce perceptions of group differences and so increase *intergroup anxiety* (or *intergroup awe*), the 'almost automatic fear' caused by interacting with members of outgroups?[27] The research evidence suggests otherwise: intergroup contact has typically and repeatedly been shown to *reduce* intergroup threat and anxiety. For example, white people who have had contact with members of other racial/ethnic groups show lower levels of physiological stress and self-reported anxiety than white people without such intergroup experiences.[28]

HOW DOES CONTACT ACTUALLY HELP TO REDUCE PREJUDICE?

Of the 515 studies included in the meta-analysis described, some met all four of Allport's conditions, others met one to three of them, while others met none. Despite these inconsistencies, the study found a significant relationship between contact and prejudice reduction; but studies that met all four conditions did show stronger effects. The researchers concluded that Allport's conditions aren't *necessary* for positive contact effects to occur; rather, they are *facilitating* conditions that are likely to make contact more effective.[29]

Consistent with this conclusion is research into factors that function as *mediators* between intergroup contact and intergroup attitudes. Rather than contact having a direct influence on prejudice reduction, there are processes that *intervene* between contact and positive attitude change, making contact only an *indirect* influence.

In an important review of these intervening processes (another meta-analysis[30]), the researchers identified the three most investigated processes:

1 *Learning about the outgroup.* This is consistent with popular thinking in the human relations movement in the U.S. in the middle of the 20th century, the explicit idea of which was that intergroup interaction would allow different groups to see just how similar they really were. However, apart from denying any actual group differences, these well-intentioned efforts carefully avoided tackling intergroup conflict at the societal level and politically explosive issues of institutional change.
2 *Generating affective ties* by reducing intergroup anxiety (see earlier).
3 *Increasing empathy and perspective taking.* Intergroup contact, and especially close, cross-group friendships, may enable us to take the perspective of outgroup members (seeing things from their point of view) and empathize with their concerns ('putting ourselves in their shoes'). This claim is consistent with recent findings that intergroup contact can involve *self-expansion processes*, in which individuals broaden their sense of self to include the outgroup. (This is related to *self-verification*, which is discussed in what follows.)

While the meta-analysis found evidence for all three processes, the researchers concluded that *affective* factors, such as anxiety reduction and empathy, are major mediators relative to more *cognitive*-oriented mediators of knowledge. This is consistent with the growing research literature on the central role of affect in intergroup processes in general and intergroup contact in particular. It also echoes what we noted in Chapter 1 regarding the greater influence of hostility and antipathy compared with negative stereotypes as influences on discriminatory behaviour. The researchers suggest that there may be a *causal sequence* involved, whereby initial anxiety must first be reduced through intergroup contact before empathy, perspective taking and knowledge of the outgroup can effectively contribute to prejudice reduction:

Intergroup contact → anxiety reduction →
empathy/perspective taking/knowledge → prejudice reduction

According to *self-verification theory* (SVT),[31] people prefer others to see them in the same way they see themselves. People base their self-concept/identity on how others treat them (as in the 'looking glass theory' of self[32]). Through our self-concept we make predictions about the world, guide our behaviour, and maintain the perception that the world is knowable and coherent. These functions make people highly motivated to maintain their identity – even if it is negative.

In turn, maintenance of our personal identity (*self-verification*) is enhanced by verification of the *ingroup identity*; this refers to qualities of typical ingroup members that may or may not characterize individual group members.[33] Thus, verification of ingroup identity represents the overlap between (a) how ingroup members perceive their group and (b) how they think that the source (outgroup members in the context of intergroup interaction) perceives the ingroup. The greater the overlap between (a) and (b), the higher the verification of ingroup identity (VII).

Research has shown that people strive to verify qualities of typical ingroup members (engage in 'the verification of group identities') even when they themselves don't possess these qualities and even when such qualities are negative. Importantly, people prefer to interact with and evaluate more positively those who confirm their group identities than those who disconfirm them.[34] Spanish high school students were asked about their contact with immigrants living in Spain: what kind of contact did they have, how did they think the immigrants perceive native Spaniards, how did they perceive Spaniards themselves and how did they generally evaluate immigrants. VII was defined and measured as the overlap between (a) how the students think that immigrants perceive Spaniards (*meta-stereotype*) and (b) how students themselves perceive Spaniards (*ingroup stereotype*): the higher the overlap, the higher the VII. As predicted, not only did VII increase positive evaluation of the outgroup, but it also lasted over time (i.e. *longitudinally*).

Why should VII mediate the effect of intergroup contact on intergroup attitudes? Two possible mechanisms are:

1 it might make individuals conscious that in the same way they stereotype the outgroup, the outgroup also stereotypes the ingroup. Being conscious of the fact that the outgroup perceives the ingroup in a similar way that they see themselves would increase intergroup trust or intergroup empathy and/or reduce anxiety;

2 ingroup individuals might perceive the outgroup as more intelligent or insightful than they expected, because they possess the capacity to think about the ingroup.[35]

CONTACT EFFECTS OR PREJUDICE EFFECTS?

Consistent with the original CH, not only does intergroup contact have long-lasting effects, but it is what produces prejudice reduction; this *contact effect* is contrasted with the *prejudice effect*, whereby prejudice leads to contact reduction (*prejudice effects*: segregation, avoidance, etc.).

A large-scale study that tested the contact effect involved more than 1,600 high school students from Belgium, England and Germany (just over 500 from ethnic minorities and the rest from ethnic majorities); intergroup contact was defined in terms of intergroup friendships.[36] The findings supported and extended previous research on the effects of outgroup friendships. Evidence was found for both contact effects and prejudice effects, and in both cases, these persisted over time. Also, contact effects were strengthened if outgroup friends were seen as highly typical of their group; they were partially mediated by intergroup anxiety. Further, contact effects were stronger for majority than minority members; indeed, for the latter they were non-existent.

This last finding has important practical implications. The overall conclusion that friendship contact doesn't work in the expected way for members of ethnic minorities has some profound implications for social policy and the design of intervention programs. Special care should be given to the way in which outgroup contact is perceived and interpreted by students from an ethnic minority background. Contact may not be beneficial if outgroup friends aren't seen as typical, even if it's of otherwise high quality and experienced as positive; similarly, if every majority member who engages in friendship contact is automatically defined as an atypical group member, contact remains ineffective.[37]

THE IMPORTANCE OF GROUP SALIENCE

As we noted, the *typicality* of both ingroup and outgroup members appears to be necessary if there's to be any chance of the positive feelings for outgroup members generalizing to the whole outgroup. This relates to *group* (or *category*) *salience* (or relevance). If categories are salient, then the respective group members are more likely to be seen as representative (or typical) of their groups, and any change in attitude towards them will then be associated with the group as a whole.[38] A number of studies have shown that, indeed, increased category salience in co-operative interactions – usually defined as the perceived typicality of the outgroup contact persons – is reliably associated with more favourable attitudes towards the outgroup as a whole.

INTERGROUP CONTACT AND INFRAHUMANIZATION

The outcome variable in studies of the contact effect is typically one or other explicit measure of intergroup attitude, prejudice or affect. But a growing number of studies is measuring the contact effect in terms of changes in *infrahumanization* (see Chapter 1). In one such study[39] involving more than a hundred British high school students, it was found that (i) the *amount* of (self-reported) contact with a member of the outgroup predicted more favourable attitudes towards the outgroup as a whole on a range of measures of attitude change, including infrahumanization; (ii) there was a tendency for perceived typicality to moderate the relationship between contact and attitude over a period of time: there was a more positive association between quality of contact and favourable attitude for those believing that the outgroup person was highly typical of their group compared with those who saw him/her as less typical.

According to the *common ingroup identity model* (CIIM),[40] certain cognitive representations of groups act as potential mediators between positive contact and prejudice reduction. Co-operative contact should reduce the salience of group distinctions while at the same time favouring the adoption of a *superordinate identity* that includes both ingroup and outgroup. The recategorization of groups from 'us' and 'them' to a superordinate, inclusive 'we' (*common ingroup identity*) should, in turn, redirect the cognitive and motivational forces producing ingroup bias to former outgroup members. These forces should then produce positive cognitive, affective and behavioural consequences for intergroup relations.

One test of the CIIM focused on outgroup infrahumanization in the context of the relationship between Jewish (the dominant group) and Arab Israelis (the low-status group).[41] The study examined the common, superordinate identity of 'Israeli' as a moderator of outgroup infrahumanization. The researcher found that the more that Jewish students perceived Arab Israelis as self-identifying as 'Israelis', and the more that Arab students actually identified as 'Israelis', the less likely the ingroup was to attribute the outgroup with fewer secondary (i.e. uniquely human) emotions; in other words, infrahumanization was reduced when ingroup and outgroup were perceived as both belonging to the superordinate group.

Evidence also exists that both decreased outgroup anxiety and increased empathy (see earlier), associated with contact and cognitive representations, will produce greater outgroup humanization. Increased empathy may be associated with the discovery of uniquely human emotions and attributes in outgroup members; reduced anxiety may be related to perception of the outgroup as less threatening, and, therefore, to a reduced need to use infrahumanization as a strategy for justifying one's feelings of threat.[42] The researchers believe that their findings have important practical implications.

> The denial of humanness to the outgroup is a widespread phenomenon that has detrimental effects on intergroup relations . . . humanity attributions might be improved by creating optimal conditions for contact and promoting the adoption of a common identity. Enhanced attributions of humanness may promote cooperation, the acceptance of affirmative action policies, and the integration of lower-status groups.[43]

Not only does positive contact result in increased humanization of the outgroup, but outgroup humanization has been shown to lead to the desire for contact with outgroup members.

As we have noted elsewhere, infrahumanization – and dehumanization (see Chapter 1) – of an outgroup may occur as a means of avoiding feelings of guilt regarding past and/or present treatment of that group by the ingroup. A study that took advantage of real-life, naturally occurring contact between Polish and Jewish Israeli students revealed that contact that focused on contemporary issues had positive effects on both outgroup attitudes and perceived similarity to the outgroup; however, no such effects occurred when the groups discussed historical issues, specifically, Poland's involvement in the Holocaust.[44]

Strong anti-outgroup prejudice is evident – and prevalent – among members of both Jews and Poles. There have been few opportunities for contact between them since 1945, which is why Polish anti-Semitism has been described as 'anti-Semitism without Jews';[45] the same could be said about Israeli attitudes towards Poles. For most young Poles and Israelis, the basis for intergroup prejudice is how their intergroup history has been represented. However, since about 2000, Jewish youth from Israel, North America and elsewhere have been visiting sites related to the Holocaust; this has provided the opportunity for first-time contacts between Polish and Jewish youth.

The effects of intergroup contact may differ depending on whether the self is categorized as a member of a historically continuous national group (Poles vs. Jews) or as a member of a contemporary superordinate group ('the young generation' vs. 'the past generation'). Based on CIIM, research on collective guilt indicates that when historically victimized group members categorize at the most inclusive human level, they perceive genocide as more pervasive across human history, which, in turn, increases forgiveness for the perpetrator group. When past crimes are presented at the less inclusive level, it implies that the negative intergroup history persists. Thus, contact that's focused on contemporary issues should improve general intergroup attitudes by creating more inclusive intergroup perceptions: they categorize themselves as belonging to a common ingroup rather than seeing themselves as members of historically conflicted groups.

Polish students who talked about the past had to face uncomfortable truths about the ingroup's behaviour. This might cause them to minimize the harm done, to downplay Poland's involvement or to actually dehumanize past victims. Such defensive processes were found to increase negative attitudes toward contemporary outgroup members.[46]

GROUP SALIENCE AND NEGATIVE CONTACT

So far, our discussion of intergroup contact has implicitly taken this contact to be positive (as in reference to 'outgroup friendships' and the use of 'equal status', 'co-operative' etc. to describe that contact). This represents a serious *positivity bias* that has dogged most of the research that has investigated the CH.[47] In natural settings, which are often unstructured and unsupervised, intergroup contact can be either positive or *negative*; but the past focus on using intergroup contact to *improve* intergroup relations has led to the progressive exclusion of negative contact from most research studies. As a result, social psychologists have presented a more positive picture of intergroup contact than suggested by related disciplines (such as sociology, political science and human geography).[48] Recent evidence suggests that intergroup friction may persist because negative contact facilitates intergroup hostility more powerfully than positive contact facilitates harmony. In other words, negative contact seems to have a disproportionately larger impact on broad intergroup relations than positive contact because of an *asymmetrical relationship* between contact valence and category (group) salience: group memberships are more salient when contact is negative (the *valence-salience effect*/VSE[49]). For example, when describing a visibly non-white contact partner, white Australians made more frequent and earlier references to ethnicity (an indication of high ethnicity salience) if she had displayed negative (as opposed to positive or neutral) nonverbal behaviour.[50]

Negative contact causes greater attention to group memberships while the contact is taking place, and these VSEs are critical, because individuals are more likely to generalize from individual contact experiences to more general group-based responses when groups are salient. Category salience is the key cognitive gatekeeper of generalized changes in intergroup relations following contact. For there to be generalized changes in intergroup relations following intergroup contact, the contact partners must be aware of their respective group memberships, attend to intergroup differences or treat each other as representative/typical of their social groups. However, as we've noted, not all types of intergroup contact provide the same degree of category salience and hence potential to shape broad intergroup relations.[51]

One way of exploring VESs is to ask whether individual differences in *past histories* of intergroup contact can help shape the potential for present contact experiences to affect broad intergroup relations. If someone has had previous negative interactions with outgroups and similarly negative expectations about them, any later negative contact with outgroup members would increase category salience situationally: negative contact is more consistent with – has better perceived fit – with the person's negative expectations. Examples of negative contact are more easily brought to mind. These *qualitative* aspects of past contact are matched by *quantitative* aspects: *limited* experience with the outgroup is associated with perceived *group homogeneity* ('they're all the same': see earlier), more extreme outgroup attitudes, and more polarized responses to attitudinally relevant information. In contrast, individuals with *extensive* intergroup contact hold more diverse and less extreme outgroup attitudes and perceptions; this reduces the degree to which any single interaction will confirm or disconfirm expectations about interactions with outgroup members. Based on these previous findings, it was predicted that (i) VSEs would be stronger among individuals with negative or limited histories of intergroup contact; (ii) VSEs would be significantly smaller among individuals with a history of relatively more positive or extensive histories of intergroup contact. These predictions were confirmed.[52]

EXTENDING THE CH: WHAT COUNTS AS 'CONTACT'?

Despite the obvious benefits of intergroup contact, it can only reduce prejudice when social groups and group members are given the *opportunity* to interact. Unfortunately, there are many examples of problematic intergroup relations which curtail such opportunities. For example, only 5 per cent of children in Northern Ireland attend mixed Catholic–Protestant schools,[53] and in the U.S., segregation of Latino and white communities is widespread;[54] similarly, the average white person lives in a predominantly white neighbourhood with less than 10 per cent black residents.[55] More extreme and more institutionalized segregation is found in the 'West Bank Wall' in Israel and the 'Green Line' in Cyprus.[56] What all these cases show is that where intergroup contact is most needed is precisely where it's most difficult to achieve.[57]

Interestingly, in the study discussed in relation to VSEs, the researchers had some participants (Protestants and Catholics in

Northern Ireland) engage in face-to-face contact (the method used by most studies to date), while others (on Arizona's southern border) were involved in a television-mediated contact (between non-Latino participants and two Latino media characters – a Latina illegal immigrant and a Latino U.S. citizen border patrolman featured in a TV documentary). With a third group (also in Arizona), an *imagined contact* procedure was used.

While the original CH took *direct*, face-to-face contact as the 'default' mode of contact (it's what 'contact' meant in this context), recent research has adopted a number of *indirect* forms of contact. The television-mediated contact used in the study just described is referred to as *parasocial contact* (which would also subsume *electronic contact*) and, as we've seen, the study also used *imagined contact*. Another form of indirect contact is *extended contact*.

EXTENDED INTERGROUP CONTACT

Research has shown that *cross-group friendship* generates stronger positive effects than other less intimate forms of contact.[58] While this finding isn't too surprising, more surprising is the finding that even *extended intergroup contact* (EIC) – merely knowing that another ingroup member has a close relationship with an outgroup member – may lead to more positive outgroup attitudes.[59] How might extended contact have these effects?

When we get close to another person, how we represent our self comes to overlap with that person: some of his/her identities become part of our own. If the friend is an outgroup member, this inclusion of his/her identity (*inclusion of the outgroup in the self*/IOS) generalizes to the outgroup as a whole. In the case of EIC, the process takes the form of a *transitive inclusion*: from the ingroup member to his/her friend to the whole outgroup. The IOS process should attenuate the tendency to assign a different human status (infrahumanization) to the ingroup and outgroup: the two groups have become assimilated, both being parts of the self. In turn, inclusion of the outgroup in the self should increase trust and empathy and reduce outgroup anxiety (see earlier).

As expected, research has shown that IOS reduces outgroup infrahumanization both *directly* and indirectly through the *mediation* of trust, empathy and anxiety.[60]

Another mechanism associated with cross-group friendship effects relates to *norms*. To the extent that the outgroup friend is perceived as typical of the outgroup, his/her positive actions can be taken as demonstrating that the outgroup's norms are favourable to the ingroup. Similarly, in the case of EIC, knowing about friendly interactions between ingroupers and outgroupers may weaken the idea of negative outgroup norms. EIC can also lead to the conclusion that the *ingroup's* norms are favourable towards the outgroup.

An Italian study in which the outgroup were more than 200 self-reported male and female homosexuals found that cross-group friendships and EIC are related to reduced infrahumanization through two levels of mediation: (i) IOS, ingroup and outgroup norms and (ii) increased empathy and trust and reduced anxiety.[61]

IMAGINED INTERGROUP CONTACT

The claim that simply *imagining* intergroup contact with an outgroup member may be enough to produce more positive intergroup attitudes represents an important extension of the original CH. *Imagined intergroup contact* (IIC) is the mental simulation of a social interaction with a member or members of an outgroup. When people imagine an intergroup interaction, they're likely to *actively* engage in conscious processes that parallel those involved in actual intergroup contact; for example, they may think about what they'd find out about the outgroup member, how they'd feel during the interaction, and how this would influence their perceptions of that outgroup more generally.[62]

In three separate but related studies, it was shown that participants asked to imagine a positive interaction with an outgroup member subsequently expressed more positive attitudes and stereotyped less than participants who weren't.[63] Two studies showed that young participants who imagined a scenario in which they were involved in a short positive interaction with an older person showed less ingroup favouritism bias in subsequent evaluations; this was found when they were compared with other participants who either imagined an outdoor scene or simply thought about an older person (without any interaction involved). In the third study, male heterosexuals who imagined talking to a male homosexual on a train later evaluated male homosexuals in general more positively and stereotyped this group much less (were less likely to see them as 'all being the same') than participants who imagined an outdoor scene. Just as with actual intergroup contact, key mediating processes that account for the positive impact of IIC effects include reduced intergroup anxiety.[64]

While IIC provides an exciting new approach to improving intergroup attitudes, it's unlikely to produce *as* powerful effects as actual contact. Recent research has shown that actual contact is stronger at reducing prejudice than EIC.[65] IIC, being arguably more indirect than EIC, may have a weaker effect compared to actual direct contact.[66]

> Imagined contact might be highly valuable as a 'first step' on the route towards reconciliation and reduced prejudice. We therefore recommend that one of the variables that ongoing research should focus on is *intentions* to engage in future intergroup interactions.[67]

Most of the studies described have measured the effects of IIC in fairly *explicit*, self-reported ways (including the attribution of secondary emotions as in infrahumanization). But some studies have investigated the impact of IIC on *implicit* prejudice as measured by the Implicit Association Test (IAT; see Chapter 1). In the first study that claimed to show that imagining intergroup contact can reduce implicit prejudice, young participants who imagined talking to an elderly stranger subsequently showed more positive implicit attitudes towards elderly people in general; in the same study, the researchers found than non-Muslim participants who imagined talking to a Muslim stranger subsequently showed more positive implicit attitudes towards Muslims in general. (In both cases, the participants were compared with others who were asked to imagine an outdoor scene.[68])

Notwithstanding the criticisms that have been made of how results using the IAT should be interpreted (see Chapter 1), 'the findings we observed remain highly important for attempts to develop imagined contact means of improving intergroup relations'.[69]

Finally, research has shown that using the IIC method can have a positive impact on *stereotype content*. As we noted in Chapter 1, warmth and competence represent two fundamental dimensions underlying ingroup and outgroup stereotypes. According to the stereotype content model (SCM),[70] groups that are perceived as low on both dimensions are likely to be dehumanized: they're seen as not human and elicit negative emotions (such as disgust and contempt) and discriminatory behaviours (including violence).

Linking work on IIC to research based on the SCM, a study conducted in Italy aimed to see whether imagined contact could reduce intergroup hostility toward social groups that are stereotyped as low on both warmth and competence.[71] The researchers selected four immigrant groups which were representative of the largest national groups living in Italy and which were perceived differently in terms of these dimensions based on previous research: Albanians (low warmth/low competence), Canadians (high/high), Chinese (low/high) and Peruvians (high/low). The Albanians are the largest of the minority groups and are commonly perceived as criminals and deviants as well as uncivilized.

The most important single finding was that imagined contact enhanced both the perceived warmth and competence of Albanians. The overall findings (for all four minority groups) show that IIC is a valuable and effective method for reducing hostility in general, and promoting stereotype change in particular.[72]

ELECTRONIC CONTACT

The Internet (or E-*contact*) represents another form of indirect contact between ingroup and outgroup members. Research has shown that direct contact – mainly face to face – with lesbians and gay men is associated with decreased feelings of intergroup anxiety, which, in turn, is associated with reduced anti-homosexual prejudice on the part of heterosexuals.[73] Also, past research has found support for the benefits of E-contact for improving intergroup relations, such as between Muslim and Christian high school students in Australia who attended religiously segregated schools.[74]

Recently, an Australian study has brought together these two previously unrelated areas of research for the first time in order to investigate E-contact as a strategy for improving sexual minority relations and to consider the role of gender – both the heterosexual participant's and that of the homosexual interaction partner.[75]

Overall, the study showed that interacting online with a female, as opposed to a male, homosexual E-contact partner reduced heterosexual men's feelings of intergroup anxiety; this, in turn, was associated with lower anti-gay prejudice and (intentions relating to) outgroup avoidance. For heterosexual women, however, E-contact had no effect on any of these measures. What this means is that E-contact helps bring male and female heterosexuals' outgroup attitudes much closer together: heterosexual men start out as more anti-lesbian and anti-gay than heterosexual women, so they have the most to gain from positive E-contact – and the gender of the homosexual interaction partner doesn't matter.

> By providing men with the opportunity to meet a member of the outgroup in a pleasant, collaborative, and goal-oriented interaction, intergroup contact may challenge their initial intolerant beliefs about sexual minorities and, in doing so, allow for positive attitude change.
>
> Rather than being a stand-alone prejudice reduction strategy, E-contact may be a valuable introduction to intergroup contact by reducing, particularly among heterosexual men, the reluctance to engage in future contact with the sexual minority outgroup.[76]

SOME OTHER METHODS OF PREJUDICE REDUCTION

EDUCATION AND CONSCIOUSNESS-RAISING

In what's come to be called the 'blue eyes–brown eyes experiment', Jane Elliot, a teacher of nine-year-olds in the U.S., told her class one day that brown-eyed people are more intelligent and 'better' people than those with blue eyes. Despite being in the minority, brown-eyed pupils would be the 'ruling class' over the inferior blue-eyed children and be given extra privileges. The blue-eyed pupils were to be 'kept in their place' by being last in line, seated at the back of the classroom and given less break time; they also had to wear special collars as a sign of their low status.

Within a short time, the blue-eyed children's academic performance began to decline, they became depressed and angry and described themselves more negatively. The brown-eyed group became mean, oppressing the others and making derogatory comments about them.

The next day, Elliot announced that she'd made a mistake and that it was really blue-eyed people who are superior. The pattern of prejudice and discrimination quickly switched from the blue-eyed children as victims to the brown-eyed.

At the end of the experiment, Elliot debriefed the children. She told them its purpose was to provide them with an opportunity to experience the evils of prejudice and discrimination in a protected environment.[77] In a follow-up study of the children when they were 18, Elliot found that they described themselves as being more tolerant of differences between groups and actively opposed to prejudice.

Elliot's experiment demonstrates the potential impact of experiencing prejudice and discrimination firsthand. Prejudice is mindless: if we teach people, especially children, to be mindful of others, to think of them as complex, whole individuals, stereotyped responses could be reduced (but see Chapter 1).[78]

'HYPOCRISY INTERVENTION'

Log onto Twitter, open a newspaper or turn on the TV news and you'll soon see just how prevalent anti-Muslim sentiment is, as well as how likely collective blame is to be placed on Muslims as a whole for actions perpetrated by a few Islamic extremists. Despite the fact that American mass shootings are far more likely to be perpetrated by white men than by Muslims, and despite them sometimes claiming allegiance to and/or espousing the views of neo-Nazi, white suprem- acist or misogynist hate groups, these men are characterized as 'lone wolves' or disturbed individuals.[79]

A recent study has investigated the effectiveness of a simple inter- vention to reduce anti-Muslim sentiment.[80] White, Spanish par- ticipants were asked to rate how much they blamed Muslims for individual acts of violence perpetrated by extremists (specifically, the bombing of the Brussels airport in 2016). Anti-Muslim sentiments were also measured by the extent to which participants agreed with statements such as 'We should dramatically decrease the amount of aid we provide to refugees in order to deter them from trying to come to our country'.

Before completing these ratings, some of the participants received a 'collective blame hypocrisy intervention' (CBHI): they were asked to read three descriptions of violence perpetrated by white Europeans (such as the attack by Anders Breivik in Norway in 2011) and then rate how responsible they felt the group was as a whole and how responsible they *personally* were. They were then given a description of the 2015 Islamic State terror attack in Paris together with a biography of a Muslim woman who owned a bakery there and asked to consider how responsible she and others like her were.

These CBHI participants responded with an average score of 16 on the 100-point scale of collective blame, compared with the 44 of the control group (which received no intervention). The intervention group also showed reduced anti-Muslim sentiment compared to the control group.

Both groups underwent the same ratings procedure 30 days and 12 months later; the differences at the first testing were maintained, despite a large terror attack perpetrated by Muslim terrorists taking place in between times. The researchers also report that the inter- vention's effects were strongest in those who had 'preference for consistency', such that it's hypocritical to blame 'Muslims' for terrorist attacks but not 'white supremacists' or 'extreme right-wing neo-Nazis'. While we're often unaware of these kind of inconsistencies, becoming aware can lead to attitude change.

> Collective blame doesn't exist in a vacuum, and it's unlikely that a one-minute intervention will be able to undo the vast amount of social conditioning that leads people to harbour explicitly or implicitly discriminatory views. But understanding the logic behind collective blame, and developing strategies to deal with it, could be one arm in a wider fight against prejudice.[81]

CONCLUSIONS: THE NATURE OF PREJUDICE REVISITED

We began this book by considering what is meant by 'prejudice', 'discrimination' and 'bias'. We also considered prejudice as an extreme attitude, comprising three components – *stereotypes* (the *cognitive* component), (usually) *hostile feelings* (the *affective* component) and *discrimination* (the *behavioural* component). How these three components are interrelated and how they're acquired is arguably the key to understanding this universal phenomenon.

While stereotyping is an example of 'thinking in categories', which, it's generally agreed, is an inherent feature of human cognition (we cannot help but think this way), the *content* of these categories is, clearly, learned through immersion in a particular socio-cultural setting at a particular historical period. It's perhaps less clear what the source of the hostility may be, except that it's often connected to the stereotype content.

We've also noted that 'discrimination' is a generic term; the behavioural component of 'prejudice' can take many different forms, differing in both degree of intensity (and related seriousness of consequences for the victims) and their relative passivity or activity. For example, telling racial jokes is active but not as extreme as, say, being overtly aggressive towards some ethnic group that's not one's own; avoiding members of an outgroup is passive, and its consequences can vary depending on circumstances.

What's very likely is that avoidance will reinforce negative stereo-types: like the person with a fear of the dentist who doesn't go and so cannot test his/her fear against reality, so the prejudiced individual who avoids contact with outgroup members – often through an equivalent fear (which is itself bred from stereotypes which haven't been tested) – simply 'sits' on their prejudice.

The research discussed in this chapter has shown, quite convincingly, that the opportunity to test this fear against real flesh-and-blood members of outgroups is the key to reducing prejudice. However, if it's 'normal' to be, say, racially prejudiced in a racist society, then we cannot realistically hope that intergroup contact alone will eliminate prejudice altogether.

The combination of the inherent 'thinking in categories', the need for ingroup belongingness for a positive self-esteem (as claimed by social identity theory) and the reality of historical and institutional racism, sexism and so on ensure that psychologists will need to continue their research into how to combat this undesirable aspect of human behaviour for a long time to come.

FURTHER READING

Allport, G.W. (1954) *The Nature of Prejudice*. **Reading, MA: Addison-Wesley.**
This is the classic text on the psychology of prejudice, which is still cited after almost 70 years and was the original stimulus for all the intergroup contact research aimed at prejudice reduction.

Appiah, K.A. (2018) *The Lies That Bind: Rethinking Identity. Creed, Country, Colour, Class, Culture*. **London: Profile Books.**
This highly respected philosopher challenges our assumptions about how identity is created. The key to understanding ourselves is to appreciate the complexity of being human: we each have many identities, and these are subject to constant change.

Fine, C. (2010) *Delusions of Gender: The Real Science Behind Sex Differences*. **London: Icon Books.**
Written by a cognitive neuroscientist, this book is a humorous yet very serious attack on what she calls 'neurosexism', the view that gender differences in cognitive abilities and behaviour in general are caused by male–female differences in genetic makeup and brain functioning.

If you enjoy this, you'll probably also enjoy her Testosterone Rex: Unmaking the Myth of Our Gendered Minds (2017). London: Icon Books.

Rutherford, A. (2020) *How to Argue with a Racist.* London: Weidenfeld & Nicolson.

The publisher states that this is a 'vital manifesto for a twenty-first-century understanding of human evolution and variation, and a timely weapon against the misuse of science to justify bigotry'. The author provides arguments that probably many racists, as well as non-racist readers, might find quite difficult to grasp initially, but his accessible writing style and many illustrative examples make the effort well worth it.

Saini, A. (2017) *Inferior: The True Power of Women and the Science that Shows It.* London: 4th Estate.

Saini, A. (2019) *Superior: The Return of Race Science.* London: 4th Estate.

These two books complement each other, although there's very little overlap of content between them. Like Fine, in Inferior, Saini challenges deep-rooted prejudices that underpin the gender wars (or scientific sexism). In Superior, she explores the concept of race and presents a rigorous examination of the insidious and destructive nature of race science (or scientific racism). In both volumes, Saini engages brilliantly with geneticists, anthropologists, historians, psychologists and other scientists from across the globe.

NOTES

CHAPTER I

1 Littlewood and Lipsedge, 1997—3rd ed., p. 52

2 Sumner, 1906

3 Triandis, 1990

4 2nd ed., 1975

5 1987

6 Miller and Ross, 1975

7 Ross, 1977

8 Pettigrew, 1979

9 Lippman, 1922

10 Allport, 1954

11 Brown, 1986

12 Dominick and Rauch, 1972

13 Culley and Bennett, 1976

14 E.g. McArthur and Resko, 1975

15 Manstead and McCulloch, 1981

16 Ferrante et al., 1988

17 Grau and Zotos, 2016

18 Matthes et al., 2016

19 Fiske, 2004

20 Dovidio et al., 1996

21 Talaska et al., 2003

22 Allport, *op cit.*

23 Fernando, 1991

24 The discussion of television advertising demonstrates a form of discrimination, namely, *androcentrism*, which doesn't really fit Allport's model, which was focused exclusively on *racism*.

25 LaPiere, 1934

26 Pettigrew, 1959

27 Haslam and Loughnan, 2014

28 Vaes et al., 2012

29 Haslam and Loughnan, 2014, p. 401

30 Leyens et al., 2001

31 Haslam and Loughnan, *op cit.*, p. 402

32 Haslam, 2006

33 Haslam, *ibid.*

34 Harris and Fiske, 2006

35 Harris and Fiske, 2011; Fiske, 2018

36 Haslam and Loughnan, *op cit.*

37 Fiske, *op cit.*

38 Haslam and Loughnan, *op cit.*

39 Bernard et al., 2012

40 Cikara et al., 2011

41 Vaes et al., 2011

42 Riemer et al., 2019

43 Gross, 2020

44 McConahy, 1986

45 Sears and Henry, 2003

46 Gaertner et al., 2005

47 McConahy, *op cit.*

48 Henry and Sears, *op cit.*; Fiske, *op cit.*

49 Dovidio et al., 2016

50 Greenwald et al., 2009

51 Phelps et al., 2000

52 Greenwald et al., 1988

53 Jarrett, 2018

54 Greenwald et al., 1998

55 Greenwald et al., 2015

56 Forscher et al., 2017

57 Shermer, 2017

58 Kteily et al., 2015

59 Fradera, 2015

60 Bilewicz et al., 2010

61 Demoulin et al., 2004

62 Haslam et al., 2008

63 Bilewicz and Bilewicz, 2012).

64 Leyens et al., 2000, 2007

65 Loughnan et al., 2009

66 Kessler et al., 2010

67 Castono and Guner-Sorolla, 2006

68 Bilewicz and Castano, 2006).

69 Cuddy et al., 2007

70 Vollhardt, 2009

CHAPTER 2

1 Saini, 2019

2 Saini, *ibid*.

3 Saini, *ibid*., p. 50

4 Saini, *ibid*., p. 51

5 Saini, *ibid*., p. 53, emphasis added

6 Saini, *ibid*.

7 Darwin, 1859

8 Darwin, 1871

9 Darwin, *ibid*., p. 66

10 This is interesting – and ironic – given the discussion of *infrahumanization* in Chapter 1.

11 Darwin, *ibid*., p. 126

12 Fancher and Rutherford, 2012

13 Darwin, 1871, *op cit*., p. 608

14 Fancher and Rutherford, *op cit*., p. 253

15 Banton, 1987

16 Banton, *ibid*.

17 Saini *op cit*.

18 Fernando, 1991

19 Banton, *op cit*.

20 Fernando, *op cit.*

21 Kolbert, 2018.

22 Saini *op cit.*

23 Montagu, 1942

24 Saini, *ibid.*, p. 93

25 Saini, *ibid.*

26 Lewontin, 1972

27 Saini, *op cit.*

28 Fernando, *op cit.* Although this figure is lower than Lewontin's 90 per cent, their conclusions regarding the predominance of within-population differences are essentially the same.

29 Bamshad and Olson, 2003

30 Bamshad and Olson, *ibid.*

31 Kolbert *op cit.*

32 Kolbert, *ibid.*

33 Rutherford, 2020, p. 24

34 Richards, 1996

35 Wetherell, 1996, p. 184

36 Wetherell, *ibid.*

37 Saini, *op cit.*

38 Saini, *ibid.*, p. 74

39 Siani, *ibid.*

40 Saini, *ibid.*

41 Gould, 1981

42 Gould, *ibid.*, p. 233

43 Saini, *op cit.*

44 Stern, 1912

45 Gould, *op cit.*

46 Gross, 2008, p. 390

47 Gould, *op cit.* Terman was based at Stanford University, California; hence the 'Stanford-Binet' test.

48 Gould, *ibid.*

49 Boring, 1923

50 Gould, *op cit.*, p. 196

51 Gould, *ibid.*, p. 198

52 Gross, 2008, *op cit.*, p. 396

53 Deese, 1972

54 Gross, 2008, *op cit.*

55 Gardner, 1993, p. xvii

56 Segall et al., 1990

57 Miller, 1997

58 Miller, *ibid.*

59 Herrnstein and Murray, 1994

60 Cited in Kamin, 1995

61 Littlewood and Lipsedge, 1997, pp. xii–xiii

62 Littlewood and Lipsedge, *ibid.*

63 Littlewood and Lipsedge, *ibid.*, p. 27, emphasis added. Seeing these outsiders as an 'undifferentiated mass' is referred as the *outgroup homogeneity effect*: see Chapter 6.

64 Littlewood and Lipsedge, *ibid.*, p. 27. Here they're describing *dehumanization* and *infrahumanization*: see Chapter 1.

65 DSM-II, 1968

66 Davison et al., 2004

67 Kitzinger, 1990

68 DSM-III-R, 1987

69 DSM-IV, 1994

70 DSM-TR, 2000; 'TR' stands for 'text revision'

71 ICD-11, 2018–22

72 Gross, 2020, p. 733, emphasis in original

73 Heather, 1976

74 Szasz, 1962

75 Littlewood and Lipsedge, 1997

76 Szasz, 1974

77 Cartwright, 1851, cited in Fernando, *op cit.*

78 Tuke, 1858; cited in Fernando, *op cit.*

79 Fernando, *op cit.*

80 Fernando, *ibid.*, p. 116

81 Bhugra and Bhui, 2001, p. 1

82 Fernando, *op cit.*

83 Kendell, 1975

84 Fernando, *op cit.*, p. 117

85 Fernando, *ibid.*, p. 118, emphasis added

86 Gross, 1997

87 Bhugra and Bhui, *op cit.*, p. 3

88 Bhugra and Bhui, *ibid.*
89 Littlewood and Lipsedge, *op cit.*
90 Sue and Sue, 1990
91 Grant, 1994
92 Grant, *op cit.*
93 Grant, *ibid.*
94 Littlewood and Lipsedge, *op cit.*
95 Littlewood and Lipsedge, *ibid.*, p. 59
96 E.g. Perkins, 1991; Kitzinger and Perkins, 1993
97 Brown, 1992, p. 243
98 Brown, *ibid.*, p. 245
99 Sender, 1992, p. 256
100 Sender, *ibid.*
101 Sender, *ibid.*, pp. 240–241

CHAPTER 3

1 Eysenck, 1952
2 E.g. Freud, 1905/1977
3 Lippman, 1922, *op cit.*
4 Beginning with Katz and Braly, 1933, followed by Gilbert, 1951, then by Karlins et al., 1969, all involving Princeton students.
5 Asch, 1952
6 Sherif, 1966
7 Littlewood and Lipsedge, 1997, *op cit.*, p. 52
8 Brehm and Kassin, 1990, p. 176
9 Littlewood and Lipsedge, *op cit.*, p. 53
10 Reich, 1970
11 Hernton, 1969
12 Adorno et al., 1950
13 Brown, 1995
14 Billig, 1978, p. 36
15 Adorno et al., *op cit.*, p. 1
16 Adorno et al. didn't actually refer to the F-scale as the authoritarianism scale, but since it's designed to identify the kind of person the book was talking about, it's reasonable to suppose that it could also be called the authoritarianism scale – as it has in many subsequent reports: Brown, 1965; Furnham and Heaven, 1999.

17 Adorno et al., *op cit.*; Rokeach, 1948

18 Brown, 1953

19 Block and Block, 1950

20 Campbell and McCandless, 1951

21 Pettigrew, 1958

22 Meloen et al., 1988

23 Sinha and Hassan, 1975

24 Cohen and Streuning, 1962; Hanson and Blohm, 1974

25 Witt, 1989

26 Walker et al., 1993

27 Brown, 1995, *op cit.*

28 Forbes, 1985

29 Perlmutter, 1954, 1956

30 Henriques et al., 1987

31 Stainton-Rogers et al., 1995

32 Brown, 1965, *op cit.*

33 Christie et al., 1958

34 Brown, 1995, *op cit.*; Krech et al., 1962; Duckitt, 1992

35 Christie, 1954

36 Brown, 1965, *op cit.*

37 Titus, 1968

38 Shils, 1954

39 1956, 1960

40 Deutscher, 1959

41 Rokeach, 1960

42 Maykovich, 1975; it's unclear whether the study used Rokeach's Dogmatism scale or some other measure.

43 Kedem et al., 1987

44 Eysenck, 1954

45 Wilson, 1973

46 Eysenck and Wilson, 1978

47 Eaves and Eysenck, 1974; Martin et al., 1986

48 Billig, 1976

49 Rokeach, 1973

50 Billig and Cochrane, 1979

51 Altmeyer, 1981

52 Altmeyer, *ibid.*

53 Duckitt, 1992; Meloen et al., 1996; Taylor et al., 1994

54 Pratto et al., 1994; Sidanius and Pratto, 1999

55 Sidanius et al., 1996

56 Sidanius et al., 1994

57 Levin et al., 2002

58 Fiske, 2004, *op cit.*

59 Fiske, *ibid.*

60 Duckitt, 2001

61 Pratto et al., *op cit.*

62 Lerner, 1980; Lerner and Simmons, 1966

63 Gross, 2020, *op cit.*

64 Example given in Myers, 1994

65 Lerner, 1980, *op cit.*

66 Furnham and Gunter, 1984

67 Connors and Heaven, 1990

68 Wagstaff and Quirk, 1983

69 Furnham, 1982

70 Furnham and Heaven, *op cit.*, p. 121

71 Connors and Heaven, *op cit.*

72 Siegel and Siegel, 1957

73 Minard, 1952

74 Pettigrew, 1958, *op cit.*

75 Duckitt, 1988; Pettigrew, *ibid.*

76 Nakanishi, 1988

77 Brown, 1995, *op cit.*, p. 36, emphasis in original

CHAPTER 4

1 Adorno et al., *op cit.*

2 Fromm, 1942; published in 1941 in the U.S. as *Escape from Freedom*

3 Morea, 1990, p. 88

4 Dollard et al., 1939

5 Hovland and Sears, 1940

6 Davis, 1959

7 Hogg and Vaughan, 1995

8 Runciman, 1966

9 Vanneman and Pettigrew, 1972

10 Sherif, 1966

11   Sherif et al., 1961

12   Brown, 1986, *op cit.?*

13   Perry, 2018

14   Perry, *ibid.*

15   Fiske, *op cit.*

16   Fiske, *ibid.*

17   Tyerman and Spencer, 1983

18   Tyerman and Spencer, *ibid.*

19   Gross, 2020, p. 421, emphasis in original

20   Meeussen et al., 2013

21   Stephan and Stephan, 2000; this shouldn't be confused with 'stereotype' threat: see Chapter 1.

22   Tajfel and Turner, 1986

23   Meeussen et al., *op cit.*

24   Meeussen et al., *op cit.*

25   Hewstone and Brown, 1986

26   Meeussen et al., *op cit.*

27   Moghaddam et al., 2016

28   Moghaddam et al., *ibid.*, p. 415

29   Moghaddam et al., *ibid.*, p. 417

30   Amichaio-Hamburger, 2017

31   Amichai-Hamburger, *ibid.*

32   Haslam et al., 2008

33   Amichai-Hamburger, *op cit.*, p. 74

34   Amichai-Hamburger, *ibid.*, pp. 75–76

35   Allport, *op cit.*

36   These, also including newspapers, were originally referred to as the 'mass media of communication', with 'mass' being dropped once PCs became commonplace.

37   Although prejudice and discrimination weren't explicitly included in measures of media effects, we know that discrimination can take aggressive/violent forms. Also, minority group stereotypes, and gender stereotypes (see Chapter 1), as included in media content, are likely to contribute to prejudiced feelings and discriminatory behaviour.

38   Bushman and Anderson, 2001

39   Prot et al., 2016

40   Taylor et al., 1994

41   Prot et al., *op cit.*

CHAPTER 5

1 Sherif, 1966, op cit.
2 Sherif et al., op cit.
3 Brown, 1986, op cit., p. 543
4 Tyerman and Spencer, op cit.
5 Brown, 1996
6 Tajfel et al., 1971
7 Oakes, 2004
8 Billig and Tajfel, 1973; Locksley et al., 1980
9 Brown, 1988, op cit.
10 Wetherell, 1982
11 E.g. Schiffman and Wicklund, 1992
12 Tajfel, 1972
13 Oakes, 2004, p. 113, emphasis in original
14 Gross, 2008, op cit.
15 Tajfel, op cit.
16 Gross, 2008, op cit.
17 Tajfel, 1978; Tajfel and Turner, 1979, 1986
18 Brown, 1988, op cit.
19 Brown, 1996, op cit.
20 Gross, 2008, op cit.
21 Allport, op cit.
22 Tajfel, 1969; Tajfel et al., 1971
23 Howitt and Owusu-Bempah, 1994
24 Vivian and Brown, 1995
25 Brewer, 1999; Hewstone et al., 2002
26 Reicher et al., 2012
27 Hackel et al., 2014
28 This findings is related to concept of infrahumanization discussed in Chapter 1.
29 Turner, 1985; Turner et al., 1987
30 Pennington et al., 1999
31 Burr, 2002, p. 88
32 Wetherell, 1996
33 Pagel, 2012, p. 27
34 Sheskin, 2018
35 Sheskin, ibid; Starmans et al., 2017
36 Sheskin, ibid., p. 30

CHAPTER 6

1 Allport, 1954, op cit.

2 Gross, 2020

3 Bronfenbrenner, 1960

4 Quattrone, 1986

5 Linville et al., 1989

6 Gross, op cit.

7 Aronson, 1980

8 Amir, 1994

9 Deutsch and Collins, 1951

10 Stouffer et al., 1949; Amir, 1969

11 Stephan, 1978

12 Aronson, 2000

13 Pettigrew and Tropp, 2006

14 Al-Ramiah and Hewstone, 2013

15 Brown, 1986, op cit.

16 Sherif et al., op cit.

17 Aronson et al., 1978

18 Aronson, op cit.

19 Aronson, 1992; Aronson, op cit.

20 Aronson, 1992, op cit.

21 Pettigrew, 2009

22 Gaertner and Dovidio, 2000; Hewstone, 1996; New, 2013; Pettigrew, 1997

23 Tausch et al., 2010

24 Brown, 1988, op cit.

25 Hewstone, 2003

26 Harwood et al., 2003

27 Islam and Hewstone, 1993; Stephan and Stephan, 1985

28 Pettigrew and Tropp, op cit.

29 Pettigrew and Tropp, op cit.

30 Pettigrew and Tropp, 2008

31 Swann, 1983, 2011

32 Cooley, 1902

33 Gomez et al., 2013

34 Gomez et al., ibid.

35 Gomez et al., ibid.

36 Binder et al., 2009

37 Binder et al., *ibid.*

38 Brown and Hewstone, 2005

39 Brown et al., 2007

40 Gaertner and Dovidio, 2000

41 Gaunt, 2009

42 Capozza et al., 2013

43 Capozza et al., *ibid.*, p. 538; Capozza et al., 2017

44 Bilewicz, 2007

45 Lendvai, 1971

46 Lendvai, *ibid.*

47 Pettigrew and Tropp, 2006, *op cit.*; Pettigrew, 2008, *op cit.*

48 Pettigrew and Tropp, 2011

49 Paolini et al., 2010

50 Paolini et al., 2014

51 Paolini et al., *op cit.*

52 Paolini et al., 2014, *op cit.*

53 Census, 2001

54 Martin, 2006

55 Logan, 2001

56 Pettigrew, 2008

57 Crisp et al., 2008

58 Davies et al., 2011

59 Turner et al., 2007

60 Capozza et al., 2013, 2014; Vezzali et al., 2012

61 Capozza et al., 2014, *op cit.*

62 Crisp et al., 2008

63 Turner, Crisp et al., 2007

64 Turner et al., *ibid.*

65 Paolini et al., 2007; Turner, Hewstone et al., 2007

66 Crisp et al., 2008, *op cit.*

67 Crisp et al., *ibid.*, p. 10, emphasis in original

68 Turner and Crisp, 2010

69 Turner and Crisp, *ibid.*, p. 11

70 Harris and Fiske, *op cit.*

71 Brambilla et al., 2012

72 Brambilla et al., *ibid.*

73 E.g. West and Hewstone, 2012

74 White and Abu-Rayya, 2012
75 White et al., 2018
76 White et al., *ibid.*, p. 10
77 Reported in Aronson and Osherow, 1980
78 Hogg and Vaughan, 1995
79 Reynolds, 2019
80 Bruneau et al., 2019
81 Reynolds, *op cit.*, p. 2

REFERENCES

Adorno, T.W., Frenkel-Brunswick, E., Levinson, D.J. and Sanford, R.N. (1950) *The Authoritarian Personality*. New York: Harper & Row.

Al Ramiah, A. and Hewstone, M. (2013) Intergroup Contact as a Tool for Reducing, Resolving, and Preventing Intergroup Conflict: Evidence, Limitations, and Potential. *American Psychologist*, *68*(7), 527–542.

Allport, G.W. (1954) *The Nature of Prejudice*. Reading, MA: Addison-Wesley.

Altmeyer, B. (1981) *Right-wing Authoritarianism*. Winnipeg: University of Manitoba Press.

American Psychiatric Association (APA). (1968) *Diagnostic and Statistical Manual of Mental Disorders* (2nd edition). New York: APA.

American Psychiatric Association (APA). (1980) *Diagnostic and Statistical Manual of Mental Disorders* (3rd edition). New York: APA.

American Psychiatric Association (APA). (1987) *Diagnostic and Statistical Manual of Mental Disorders* (3rd edition, Revised). New York: APA.

American Psychiatric Association (APA). (1994) *Diagnostic and Statistical Manual of Mental Disorders* (4th edition). New York: APA.

American Psychiatric Association (APA). (2000) *Diagnostic and Statistical Manual of Mental Disorders* (4th edition, Text Revision). New York: APA.

American Psychiatric Association (APA). (2013) *Diagnostic and Statistical Manual of Mental Disorders* (5th edition, Text Revision). New York: APA.

Amichaio-Hamburger, Y. (2017) *Internet Psychology: The Basics*. London: Routledge.

Amir, Y. (1969) Contact hypothesis in ethnic relations. *Psychological Bulletin*, 71, 319–342.

Amir, Y. (1994) The contact hypothesis in intergroup relations. In W.J. Lonner and R.S. Malpass (eds.) *Psychology and Culture*. Boston, MA: Allyn & Bacon.

Aronson, E. (1980) *The Social Animal* (3rd edition). San Francisco: W.H. Freeman.

Aronson, E. (1992) *The Social Animal* (6th edition). New York: W.H. Freeman & Co.

Aronson, E. (2000) The jigsaw strategy: Reducing prejudice in the classroom. *Psychology Review*, 7(2), 2–5.

Aronson, E., Blaney, N., Stephan, C. et al. (1978) *The Jig-Saw Classroom*. London: Sage.

Aronson, E. and Osherow, N. (1980) Co-operation, prosocial behaviour and academic performance: Experiments in the desegregated classroom. In L. Bickman (ed.) *Applied Social Psychology Annual* (Vol. 1). Beverly, CA: Sage.

Asch, S.E. (1952) *Social Psychology*. New York: Prentice-Hall.

Bamshad, M.J. and Olson, S.E. (2003) Does race exist? *Scientific American*, 289(6), 78–85.

Banton, M. (1987) *Racial Theories*. Cambridge: Cambridge University Press.

Bernard, P., Gervais, S., Allen, J. et al. (2012) Integrating sexual objectification with object versus person recognition: The sexualized boy-inversion hypothesis. *Psychological Science*, 23, 469–471.

Bhugra, D. and Bhui, K. (2001) *Cross-Cultural Psychiatry: A Practical Guide*. London: Arnold.

Bilewicz, M. (2007) History as an obstacle: Impact of temporal-based social categorizations on Polish-Jewish intergroup contact. *Group Processes & Intergroup Relations*, 10(4), 551–563.

Bilewicz, M. and Bilewicz, A. (2012) Who defines humanity? Psychological and cultural obstacles to omniculturalism. *Culture & Psychology*, 18(3), 331–344.

Bilewicz, M. and Castano, E. (2006) *Dehumanization in the Media: Depictions of Natural Disasters in Three American Newspapers*. Unpublished research report cited in Bilewicz and Bilewicz, 2012.

Bilewicz, M., Mikolajczak, M., Kumagai, T. and Castano, E. (2010) Which emotions are uniquely human? Understanding of emotion words across three cultures. In B. Bokus (ed.) *Studies in the Psychology of Language and Communication*. Warsaw: Matrix.

Billig, M. (1976) *Social Psychology and Intergroup Relations*. London: Academic Press.

Billig, M.G. (1978) *Fascists: A Social Psychological View of the National Front*. London: Academic Press.

Billig, M.G. and Cochrane, R. (1979) Values of political extremists and potential extremists: A discriminant analysis. *European Journal of Social Psychology*, 9, 205–222.

Billig, M.G. and Tajfel, H. (1973) Social categorization and similarity in intergroup behaviour. *European Journal of Social Psychology*, 3, 27–52.

Binder, J., Zagefka, H., Brown, R. et al. (2009) Does contact reduce prejudice or does prejudice reduce contact? A longitudinal test of the contact hypothesis among majority and minority groups in three European countries. *Journal of Personality & Social Psychology*, 96(4), 843–856.

Block, J. and Block, Jeanne. (1950) An investigation of the relationship between rigidity and ethnocentrism. *Journal of Personality*, 19, 303–311.

Boring, E.G. (1923) Intelligence as the tests test it. *New Republic*, 6 June, 35–37.

Brambilla, M., Ravenna, M. and Hewstone, M. (2012) Changing stereotype content through mental imagery: Imagining intergroup contact promotes stereotype change. *Group Processes & Intergroup Relations*, 15(3), 305–315.

Brehm, S.S. & Kassin, S.M. (1990) *Social Psychology*. New York: Houghton Mifflin.

Brewer, M.B. (1999) The psychology of prejudice: Ingroup love or outgroup hate? *Journal of Social Issues*, 55, 429–444.

Bronfenbrenner, U. (1960) Freudian theories of identification and their derivatives. *Child Development*, 31, 15–40.

Brown, L.S. (1992) While waiting for the revolution: The case for a lesbian feminist psychotherapy. *Feminism & Psychology*, 2(2), 239–253.

Brown, Roger (1965) *Social Psychology*. New York: Free Press.

Brown, Roger (1986) *Social Psychology: The Second Edition*. New York: The Free Press.

Brown, Roland W. (1953) A determinant of the relationship between rigidity and authoritarianism. *Journal of Abnormal & Social Psychology*, 48, 469–476.

Brown, Rupert (1988) *Group Processes*. Oxford: Blackwell Publishing.

Brown, Rupert (1995) *Prejudice: Its Social Psychology*. Oxford: Blackwell.

Brown, Rupert (1996) Intergroup relations. In M. Hewstone, W. Stroebe and G.M. Stephenson (eds.) *Introduction to Social Psychology* (2nd edition). Oxford: Blackwell Publishing.

Brown, Rupert, Eller, A., Leeds, S. and Stace, K. (2007) Intergroup contact and intergroup attitudes: A longitudinal study. *European Journal of Social Psychology*, 37, 692–703.

Brown, Rupert and Hewstone, M. (2005) An integrative theory of intergroup contact. *Advances in Experimental Social Psychology*, 37, 255–343.

Bruneau, E.G., Kteily, N.S. and Urbiola, A. (2019) A collective blame hypocrisy intervention enduringly reduces hostility towards Muslims. *Nature Human Behaviour*. www.nature.com/articles/s41562-019-1747-7

Burr, V. (2002) *The Person in Social Psychology*. Hove: Psychology Press.

Bushman, B.J. and Anderson, C.A. (2001) Media violence and the American public. *American Psychologist*, 56, 477–489.

Campbell, D.T. and McCandless, B.R. (1951) Ethnocentrism, xenophobia, and personality. *Human Relations*, 4, 185–192.

Capozza, D., Di Bernardo, G. and Falvo, R. (2017) Intergroup contact and outgroup humanization: Is the causal relationship uni- or bidirectional? https://doi.org/10.1371/journal.pone.0170554

Capozza, D., Falvo, R., Di Bernardo, G. et al. (2014) Intergroup contact as a strategy to improve humanness attributions: A review of studies. *TPM*, 21(3), 349–362. Special Issue.

Capozza, D., Trifiletti, E., Vezzali, L. and Favara, I. (2013) Can intergroup contact improve humanity attributions? *International Journal of Psychology*, 48(4), 527–541.

Castono, E. and Guner-Sorolla, R. (2006) Not quite human: Infrahumanization in response to collective responsibility for intergroup killing. *Journal of Personality & Social Psychology*, 90, 804–818.

Census (2001) *National Statistics Government Website: Neighbourhood Statistics*. http://neighbourhood.statistics.gov.uk

Christie, R. (1954) Authoritarianism re-examined. In R. Christrie and M. Jahoda (eds.) *Studies in the Scope and Method of 'the Authoritarian Personality'*. Glencoe, IL: Free Press.

Christie, R., Havel, J. and Seidenberg, B. (1958) Is the F-scale irreversible? *Journal of Abnormal & Social Psychology*, 56, 143–159.

Cikara, M., Eberhardt, J. and Fiske, S.T. (2011) From agents to objects: Sexist attitudes and neural responses to sexualized targets. *Journal of Cognitive Neuroscience*, 3, 540–551.

Cohen, J. and Streuning, E.L. (1962) Opinions about mental illness. *Journal of Abnormal & Social Psychology*, 64, 349–360.

Connors, J. and Heaven, P. (1990) Belief in a just world and attitudes towards AIDS sufferers. *Journal of Social Psychology*, 130, 559–560.

Cooley, C.H. (1902) *Human Nature and the Social Order*. London: Transaction Publishers.

Crisp, R.J., Stathi, S., Turner, R.N. and Husnu, S. (2008) Imagined intergroup contact: Theory, paradigm and practice. *Social & Personality Psychology Compass*, 2. doi:10.1111/j.1751-9004.2008.00155x

Cuddy, A., Rock, M. and Norton, M. (2007) Aid in the aftermath of Hurricane Katrina: Inferences of secondary emotions and intergroup helping. *Group Processes and Intergroup Relations*, 10, 107–118.

Culley, J.D. and Bennett, R. (1976) Selling women, selling blacks. *Journal of Communication*. https://doi.org/10.1111/j.1460-2466.1976.tb01954.x

Darwin, C.R. (1859) *The Origin of Species by Natural Selection*. London: John Murray.

Darwin, C.R. (1871) *The Descent of Man and Selection in Relation to Sex*. London: John Murray.

Davies, K., Tropp, L.R., Aron, A. et al. (2011) Cross group friendships and intergroup attitudes: A meta-analytic review. *Personality & Social Psychology Review*, 15, 332–351.

Davis, J.A. (1959) A formal interpretation of the theory of relative deprivation. *Sociometry*, 22, 280–296.

Davison, G.C., Neale, J.M. and Kring, A.M. (2004) *Abnormal Psychology* (9th edition). New York: John Wiley & Sons Inc.

Deese, J. (1972) *Psychology as Science and Art*. New York: Harcourt Brace Jovanovich.

Demoulin, S., Torres, R.R., Perez, A.R. et al. (2004) Emotional prejudice can lead to infra-humanization. *European Review of Social Psychology*, 15, 259–296.

Deutsch, M. and Collins, M. (1951) *Interracial Housing: A Psychological Evaluation of a Social Experiment*. Minneapolis, MN: University of Minnesota Press.

Deutscher, I. (1959) *The Prophet Unarmed: Trotsky 1921–1229*. London: Oxford University Press.

Dollard, J., Doob, L.W., Mowrer, O.H. and Sears, R.R. (1939) *Frustration and Aggression*. New Haven, CT: Harvard University Press.

Dominick, J.R. and Rauch, G.E. (1972) The image of women in network TV commercials. *Journal of Broadcasting*, 16, 259–265.

Dovidio, J.F., Brigham, J.C., Johnson, B.T. and Gaertner, S.L. (1996) Stereotyping, prejudice and discrimination: Another look. In C.N. McCrae, C. Stangor and M. Hewstone (eds.) *Stereotypes and Stereotyping*. New York: Guilford.

Dovidio, J.F., Gaertner, S.L. and Pearson, A.R. (2016) Racism among the well intentioned. In A.G. Miller (ed.) *The Social Psychology of Good and Evil* (2nd edition). New York: The Guilford Press.

Duckitt, J. (1988) Normative conformity and racial prejudice in South Africa. *Genetic, Social & General Psychology Monographs*, 114, 413–437.

Duckitt, J. (1992) *The Social Psychology of Prejudice*. New York: Praeger.

Duckitt, J. (2001) A dual-process cognitive-motivational theory of ideology and prejudice. In M.P. Zanna (ed.) *Advances in Experimental Social Psychology* (Vol. 33). San Diego, CA: Academic Press.

Eaves, L.J. and Eysenck, H.J. (1974) Genetics and the development of social attitudes. *Nature*, 249, 288–289.

Eysenck, H.J. (1952) *The Scientific Study of Personality*. London: Routledge & Kegan Paul.

Eysenck, H.J. (1954) *The Psychology of Politics*. London: Routledge & Kegan Paul.

Eysenck, H.J. and Wilson, G. (1978) *The Psychological Basis of Ideology*. Lancaster: MTP Press.

Fancher, R.E. and Rutherford, A. (2012) *Pioneers of Psychology* (4th edition). New York: W.W. Norton & Co. Inc.

Fernando, S. (1991) *Mental Health, Race and Culture*. Basingstoke: Macmillan/Mind Publications.

Ferrante, C.L., Haynes, A.M. and Kingsley, S.M. (1988) Image of women in television advertising. *Journal of Broadcasting & Electronic Media*, 32(2), 231–237.

Fiske, S.T. (2004) *Social Beings: A Core Motives Approach to Social Psychology*. New York: Wiley.

Fiske, S.T. (2018) Stereotype content: Warmth and competence endure. *Current Directions in Psychological Science*, 27(2), 67–73.

Forbes, H.D. (1985) *Nationalism, Ethnocentrism, and Personality*. Chicago: University of Chicago Press.

Forscher, P.S., Lai, C., Axt, J. et al. (2017) *A Meta-Analysis of Change in Implicit Bias*. Unpublished manuscript, Department of Psychology, University of Wisconsin.

Fradera, A. (2015) *Psychologists Reveal Our 'Blatant Dehumanization' of Minority Groups*. https://digest.bps.org.uk/2015/07/24/psychologists-reveal-our-blatant-dehumanization-of-minority-groups/

Freud, S. (1905/1977) *Three Essays on the Theory of Sexuality, Pelican Freud Library* (Vol. 7). Harmondsworth: Penguin.

Fromm, E. (1942) *The Fear of Freedom*. London: RKP.

Furnham, A. (1982) Why are the poor always with us? Explanations for poverty in Britain. *British Journal of Social Psychology*, 21, 311–322.

Furnham, A. and Gunter, B. (1984) Just world beliefs and attitudes towards the poor. *British Journal of Social Psychology*, 23, 265–269.

Furnham, A. and Heaven, P. (1999) *Personality and Social Behaviour*. London: Arnold.

Gaertner, S.L. and Dovidio, J.F. (2000) *Reducing Intergroup Bias: The Common Ingroup Identity Model*. Philadelphia, PA: Psychology Press.

Gaertner, S.L., Dovidio, J.F., Nier, J. et al. (2005) Aversive racism: Bias without intention. In L.B. Nilesen and R.L. Nelson (eds.) *Handbook of Employment Discrimination Research*. New York: Springer.

Gardner, H. (1993) *Frames of Mind* (2nd edition). London: Fontana.

Gaunt, R. (2009) Superordinate categorization as a moderator of mutual infrahumanization. *Group Processes & Intergroup Relations*, 12(6), 731–746.

Gilbert, G.M. (1951) Stereotype persistence and change among college students. *Journal of Abnormal & Social Psychology*, 46, 245–254.

Gomez, A., Eller, A. and Vazquez, A. (2013) Verification of ingroup identity as a longitudinal mediator between intergroup contact and outgroup evaluation. *Spanish Journal of Psychology*, 16, e74, 1–11.

Gould, S.J. (1981) *The Mismeasure of Man*. New York: Norton.

Grant, P. (1994) Psychotherapy and trace. In P. Clarkson and M. Pokorny (eds.) *The Handbook of Psychotherapy*. London: Routledge.

Grau, L.G. and Zotos, Y. (2016) Gender stereotypes in advertising: A review of current research. *International Journal of Advertising*, 35(5), 761–770.

Greenwald, A.G., Banaji, M.R. and Nosek, B.A. (2015) Statistically small effects of the implicit association test can have societally large effects. *Journal of Personality & Social Psychology*, 108, 553–561.

Greenwald, A.G., McGhee, D.E. and Schwartz, J.K.L. (1998) Measuring individual differences in implicit cognition: The implicit association test. *Journal of Personality & Social Psychology*, 74, 1464–1480.

Greenwald, A.G., Poehlman, T.A., Uhlmann, E. and Banaji, M.R. (2009) Understanding and using the implicit association test: III. Meta-analysis of predictive validity. *Journal of Personality & Social Psychology*, 97, 17–41.

Gross, R. (2008) *Key Studies in Psychology* (5th edition). London: Hodder Education.

Gross, R. (2020) *Psychology: The Science of Mind and Behaviour* (8th edition). London: Hodder Education.

Hackel, L.M., Looser, C.E. and Van Bavel, J.J. (2014) Group membership alters the threshold for mind perception: The role of social identity, collective identification, and intergroup threat. *Journal of Experimental Social Psychology*, 52, 15–23.

Hanson, D.J. and Blohm, E.R. (1974) Authoritarianism and attitudes towards mental patients. *International Behavioural Scientist*, 6, 57–60.

Harris, L. and Fiske, S. (2006) Dehumanizing the lowest of the low: Neuroimaging responses to extreme out-groups. *Psychological Science*, 17, 847–853.

Harris, L. and Fiske, S. (2011) Dehumanized perception: A psychological means to facilitate atrocities, torture, and genocide? *Journal of Psychology*, 219, 175–181.

Harwood, J., Hewstone, M., Paolini, S. and Hurd, R. (2003) *Intergroup Contact Theory, the Grandparent-Grandchild Relationship, and Attitudes Towards Older Adults*. Manuscript submitted for publication (cited in Hewstone, 2003).

Haslam, A., Kashima, Y., Loughnan, S. et al. (2008) Subhuman, inhuman, and superhuman: Contrasting humans with nonhumans in three cultures. *Social Cognition*, 26, 248–258.

Haslam, N. (2006) Dehumanization: An integrative review. *Personality & Social Psychology Review*, 10(3), 252–264.

Haslam, N. and Loughnan, S. (2014) Dehumanization and infrahumanization. *Annual Review of Psychology*, 65, 399–423.

Heather, N. (1976) *Radical Perspectives in Psychology*. London: Longman.

Henriques, J., Hollway, W., Urwin, C. et al. (1987) *Changing the Subject: Psychology, Social Regulation and Subjectivity*. London: Methuen.

Hernton, C.C. (1969) *Sex and Racism*. London: Andre Deutsch.

Herrnstein, R.J. and Murray, C. (1994) *The Bell Curve: Intelligence and Class Structure in American Life*. New York: Free Press.

Hewstone, M. (1996) Contact and categorization: Social psychological interventions to change intergroup relations. In C.N. Macrae, C. Stangor and M. Hewstone (eds.) *Stereotypes and Stereotyping*. New York: Guilford Press.

Hewstone, M. (2003) Intergroup contact: Panacea for prejudice? *The Psychologist*, 16(7), 352–355.

Hewstone, M. and Brown, R. (1986) Contact is not enough: An intergroup perspective on the 'contact hypothesis'. In M. Hewstone and R. Brown (eds.) *Contact and Conflict in Intergroup Encounters*. Oxford: Blackwell.

Hewstone, M., Rubin, N. and Willis, H. (2002) Intergroup bias. *Annual Review of Psychology*, 53, 575–604.

Hogg, M.A. and Vaughan, G.M. (1995) *Social Psychology: An Introduction*. Hemel Hempstead: Prentice-Hall/Harvester Wheatsheaf.

Hovland, C. and Sears, R.R. (1940) Minor studies in aggression: VI: Correlation of lynchings with economic indices. *Journal of Psychology*, 9, 301–310.

Howitt, D. and Owusu-Bempah, J. (1994) *The Racism of Psychology: Time for Change*. Hemel Hempstead: Harvester Wheatsheaf.

Islam, R.M. and Hewstone, M. (1993) Dimension of contact as predictors of intergroup anxiety, perceived outgroup variability and outgroup attitudes: An integrative model. *Personality & Social Psychology Bulletin*, 19, 700–710.

Jarrett, C. (2018) *Seeing Others as Less than Human*. https://digest.bps.org/2006/11/10/seeing-otehrs-as-less-than-human

Kamin, L.J. (1995) Behind the curve. *Scientific American*, 272(2), 82–86.

Karlins, M., Coffman, T.L. and Walters, G. (1969) On the fading of social stereotypes: Studies in three generations of college students. *Journal of Personality & Social Psychology*, 13, 1–16.

Katz, D. and Braly, K. (1933) Racial stereotypes of one hundred college students. *Journal of Abnormal & Social Psychology*, 28, 280–290.

Kedem, P., Bihu, A. and Cohen, Z. (1987) Dogmatism, ideology, and right-wing radical activity. *Political Psychology*, 8, 35–47.

Kendell, R. (1975) *Role of Diagnosis in Psychiatry*. Oxford: Blackwell.

Kessler, T., Mummendey, A. and Funke, F. (2010) We all live in Germany but . . . ingroup projection, group-based emotions, and prejudice against immigrants. *European Journal of Social Psychology*, 40, 985–997.

Kitzinger, C. (1990) Heterosexism in psychology. *The Psychologist*, 3(9), 391–392.

Kitzinger, C. and Perkins, R. (1993) *Changing Our Minds: Lesbian Feminism and Psychology*. London: Onlywomen Press Ltd.

Kolbert, E. (2018) Skin deep. *National Geographic*, 233(4), 28–45.

Krech, D., Krutchfield, R.S. and Ballachey, E.L. (1962) *Individual in Society*. New York: McGraw-Hill.

Kteily, N., Bruneau, E., Waytz, A. and Cotterill, S. (2015) The ascent of man: Theoretical and empirical evidence for blatant dehumanization. *Journal of Personality & Social Psychology*. doi:10.1037/pspp0000048

LaPiere, R.T. (1934) Attitudes versus action. *Social Forces*, 13, 230–237.

Lendvai, P. (1971) *Anti-Semitism Without Jews: Communist Eastern Europe*. New York: Doubleday.

Lerner, M. (1980) *The Belief in a Just World: A Fundamental Delusion*. New York: Plenum.

Lerner, M. and Simmons, C. (1966) Observers' reactions to the 'innocent victim': Comparison or rejection? *Journal of Personality & Social Psychology*, 4, 203–210.

Levin, S., Federico, C.M., Sidanius, J. and Rabinowitz, J.L. (2002) Social dominance orientation and intergroup bias: The legitimation of favouritism for high-status groups. *Personality & Social Psychology Bulletin*, 28, 144–157.

Lewontin, R.C. (1972) The apportionment of human diversity. *Evolutionary Biology*, 6, 381–398.

Leyens, J.P., Demoulin, S., Vaes, J., Gaunt, R. and Paladino, M.P. (2007) Infrahumanization: The wall of group differences. *Social Issues & Policy Review*, 1, 139–172.

Leyens, J.P., Paladino, P.M., Rodriguez-Torres, R. et al. (2000) The emotional side of prejudice: The attribution of secondary emotions to ingroups and outgroups. *Personality & Social Psychology Review*, 4, 186–197.

Leyens, J.P., Rodriguez-Torres, A., Rodriguez-Torres, A. et al (2001) Psychological essentialism and the differential attribution of uniquely human emotions to ingroups and outgroups. *European Journal of Social Psychology*, 31, 395–411.

Linville, P.W., Fischer, F.W. and Salovey, P. (1989) Perceived distributions of characteristics of ingroup and outgroup members: Empirical evidence and a computer simulation. *Journal of Personality & Social Psychology*, 42, 193–211.

Lippman, W. (1922) *Public Opinion*. New York: Harcourt Brace.

Littlewood, R. and Lipsedge, M. (1989) *Aliens and Alienists: Ethnic Minorities and Psychiatry* (2nd edition). London: Unwin Hyman Ltd.

Littlewood, R. and Lipsedge, M. (1997) *Aliens and Alienists: Ethnic Minorities and Psychiatry* (3rd edition). London: Routledge.

Locksley, A., Borgida, E., Brekke, N. and Hepburn, C. (1980) Sex stereotypes and social judgement. *Journal of Personality & Social Psychology*, 39, 821–831.

Logan, J. (2001) *Ethnic Diversity Grows, Neighbourhood Integration Lags Behind*. Albany, NY: State University of New York, Lewis Mumford Centre.

Loughnan, S., Haslam, N. and Kashima, Y. (2009) Understanding the relationship between attribute-based and metaphor-based dehumanization. *Group Processes and Intergroup Relations*. https://doi.org/10.1177/1368430209347726

Manstead, A.S.R. and McCulloch, C. (1981) Sex-role stereotyping in British television advertisements. *British Journal of Social Psychology*, 20, 171–180.

Martin, M.E. (2006) *Residential Segregation Patterns of Latinos in the United States, 1990–2000*. New York: Routledge.

Martin, W., Eaves, L.J., Heath, A.C. et al. (1986) Transmission of social attitudes. *Proceedings of the National Academy of Science*, 83, 4364–4368.

Matthes, J., Prieler, M. and Adam, K. (2016) Gender-role portrayals in television advertising across the globe. *Sex Roles*, *75*(7), 314–327.

Maykovich, M.K. (1975) Correlates of racial prejudice. *Journal of Personality & Social Psychology*, 32, 1014–1020.

McArthur, L.Z. and Resko, B.G. (1975) The portrayal of men and women in American television commercials. *Journal of Social Psychology*, 97, 209–220.

McConahy, J.B. (1986) Self-interest versus racial attitudes as correlates of anti-busing attitudes in Louisville: Is it the buses or the blacks? *Journal of Politics*, 44, 692–720.

Meeussen, L., Phalet, K., Meeus, J. et al. (2013) 'They are all the same'. Low perceived typicality and outgroup disapproval as buffers of intergroup threat in mass media. *International Journal of Intercultural Relations*, 37, 146–158.

Meloen, J.D., Hagendoorn, L., Raaijmakers, Q. and Visser, L. (1988) Authoritarianism and the revival of political racism: Reassessments in the Netherlands of the reliability and validity of the concept of authoritarianism by Adorno et al. *Political Psychology*, 9, 413–429.

Meloen, J.D., Van der Linden, G. & De Witte, H. (1996) A test of the approaches of Adorno et al, Lederer, and Altmeyer of authoritarianism in Belgian Flanders. *Political Psychology*, 17, 643–656.

Miller, D.T. and Ross, M. (1975) Self-serving biases in the attribution of causality: Fact or fiction? *Psychological Bulletin*, 82, 213–225.

Miller, J. (1997) Theoretical issues in cultural psychology. In J.W. Berry, Y.H. Poortinga and J. Pandey (eds.) *Handbook of Cross-Cultural Research,Volume 1:Theory and Method*. Boston, MA: Allyn & Bacon.

Minard, R.D. (1952) Race relations in the Pocahontas coalfield. *Journal of Social Issues*, 8, 29–44.

Moghaddam, F.M., Heckenlaible, V., Blackman, M. et al. (2016) Globalization and terrorism: The primacy of collective processes. In A.G. Miller (ed.) *The Social Psychology of Good and Evil*. New York: The Guilford Press.

Montagu, A. (1942) *Man's Most Dangerous Myth:The Fallacy of Race*. New York: Columbia University Press.

Morea, P. (1990) *Personality:An Introduction to the Theories of Psychology*. Harmondsworth: Penguin.

Myers, D.G. (1994) *Exploring Social Psychology*. New York: McGraw-Hill.

Nakanishi, D.T. (1988) Seeking convergence in race relations research: Japanese-Americans and the resurrection of the internment. In P.A. Katz and D. Taylor (eds.) *Eliminating Racism: Profiles in Controversy*. New York: Plenum.

New, R. (2013) The social psychology of prejudice. *Psychology Review*, 19(1), 2–4.

Oakes, P. (2004) The root of all evil in intergroup relations? Unlearning the categorization process. In M.B. Brewer and M. Hewstone (eds.) *Social Cognition*. Oxford: Blackwell Publishing.

Oxford Illustrated Dictionary (1975) (2nd edition).

Pagel, M. (2012) *Wired for Culture: The Natural History of Human Cooperation*. London: Penguin Books.

Paolini, S., Harwood, J. and Rubin, M. (2010) Negative intergroup contact makes group memberships salient: Explaining why intergroup conflict endures. *Personality & Social Psychology Bulletin*, 36, 1723.

Paolini, S., Harwood, J., Rubin, M. et al. (2014) Positive and extensive intergroup contact in the past buffers against the disproportionate impact of negative contact in the present. *European Journal of Social Psychology*. doi:10.1002/ejsp.2029

Paolini, S., Hewstone, M. and Cairns, E. (2007) Direct and indirect intergroup friendship effects: Testing the moderating role of the affective-cognitive bases of prejudice. *Personality & Social Psychology Bulletin*, 33, 1406–1420.

Pennington, D., Gillen, K. and Hill, P. (1999) *Social Psychology*. London: Hodder Arnold.

Perkins, R. (1991) Therapy for lesbians? The case against. *Feminism & Psychology*, 1(3), 325–338.

Perlmutter, H.V. (1954) Some characteristics of the xenophilic personality. *Journal of Psychology*, 38, 291–300.

Perlmutter, H.V. (1956) Correlates of two types of xenophilic orientation. *Journal of Abnormal & Social Psychology*, 52, 130–135.

Perry, G. (2018) Real-life lord of the flies. *New Scientist*, 237(3165), 41–43.

Pettigrew, T.F. (1958) Personality and sociocultural factors in intergroup attitudes: A cross-national comparison. *Journal of Conflict Resolution*, 2, 29–42.

Pettigrew, T.F. (1959) Regional difference in antinegro prejudice. *Journal of Abnormal & Social Psychology*, 59, 28–56.

Pettigrew, T.F. (1979) The ultimate attribution error: Extending Allport's cognitive analysis of prejudice. *Personality & Social Psychology Bulletin*, 5, 461–476.

Pettigrew, T.F. (1997) Generalized intergroup contact effects on prejudice. *Personality & Social Psychology Bulletin*, 23, 173–185.

Pettigrew, T.F. (2008) Future direction for intergroup contact theory and research. *International Journal of Intercultural Relations*, 32, 187–199.

Pettigrew, T.F. (2009) Secondary transfer effect of contact: Do intergroup contact effects spread to noncontacted outgroups? *Social Psychology*, 40(2), 55–65.

Pettigrew, T.F. and Tropp, L.R. (2006) A meta-analytic test of intergroup contact theory. *Journal of Personality & Social Psychology*, 90(5), 751–783.

Pettigrew, T.F. and Tropp, L.R. (2008) How does intergroup contact reduce prejudice? Meta-analytic tests of three mediators. *European Journal of Social Psychology*, 38, 922–934.

Pettigrew, T.F. and Tropp, L.R. (2011) *When Groups Meet: The Dynamics of Intergroup Contact, Essays in Social Psychology*. New York: Psychology Press.

Phelps, E.A., O'Connor, K.J., Cunningham, W.A. et al. (2000) Performance on indirect measures of race evaluation predicts amygdala activation. *Journal of Cognitive Neuroscience*, 12, 729–738.

Pratto, F., Sidanius, J., Stallworth, L.M. and Malle, B.F. (1994) Social dominance orientation: A personality variable predicting social and political attitudes. *Journal of Personality & Social Psychology*, 67, 741–763.

Prot, S., Anderson, C.A., Saleem, M. et al. (2016) Understanding media violence effects. In A.G. Miller (ed.) *The Social Psychology of Good and Evil*. New York: The Guilford Press.

Quattrone, G.A. (1986) On the perception of a group's variability. In S. Worchel and W. Austin (eds.) *Social Psychology of Intergroup Relations*. Chicago: Nelson.

Reader's Digest Universal Dictionary (1987).

Reich, W. (1970) *The Mass Psychology of Fascism*. Harmondsworth: Penguin.

Reicher, S., Haslam, S.A., Spears, R. and Reynolds, K.J. (2012) A social mind: The context of John Turner's work and its influence. *European Review of Social Psychology*, 23, 344–385.

Reynolds, E. (2019) *Simple 'Hypocrisy Intervention' Reduces Collective Blaming of Muslims for Extremism, with Long-Lasting Effects*. https://digest.bps.org.uk/2019/10/22/simple-hypocrisy-intervention-reduces-collective-blaming-of-muslims-for-extremism-with-log-lasting-effects

Richards, G. (1996) Arsenic and old race. *Observer Review*, 5 May, 4.

Riemer, A.R., Gervais, S.J., Skorinko, J.L.M. et al. (2019) She looks like she'd be an animal in bed: Dehumanization of drinking women in social contexts. *Sex Roles*, 80(9–10), 617–629.

Rokeach, M. (1948) Generalized mental rigidity as a factor in ethnocentrism. *Journal of Abnormal & Social Psychology*, 43, 259–278.

Rokeach, M. (1956) Political and religious dogmatism: An alternative to the authoritarian personality. *Psychological Monographs*, 70, Whole no. 18.

Rokeach, M. (1960) *The Open and Closed Mind*. New York: Basic Books.

Rokeach, M. (1973) *The Nature of Human Values*. New York: Free Press.

Ross, L. (1977) The intuitive psychologist and his shortcomings. In L. Berkowitz (ed.) *Advances in Experimental Social Psychology* (Vol. 10). New York: Academic Press.

Runciman, W.G. (1966) *Relative Deprivation and Social Justice*. London: Routledge & Kegan Paul.

Rutherford, A. (2020) The facts about race. *The Observer*, 26 January, 23–25.

Saini, A. (2019) *Superior: The Return of Race Science*. London: 4th Estate.

Schiffman, R. and Wicklund, R.A. (1992) The minimal group paradigm and its minimal psychology. *Theory & Psychology*, 2(1), 29–50.

Sears, D.O. and Henry, P.J. (2003) The origins of symbolic racism. *Journal of Personality & Social Psychology*, 85, 259–275.

Segall, M.H., Dasen, P.R., Berry, J.W. and Poortinga, Y.H. (1990) *Human Behaviour in Global Perspective: An Introduction to Cross-Cultural Psychology*. New York: Pergamon.

Sender, K. (1992) Lesbians, therapy and politics: Inclusion and diversity. *Feminism & Psychology*, 2(2), 255–257.

Sherif, M. (1966) *Group Conflict and Co-Operation: Their Social Psychology*. London: Routledge and Kegan Paul.

Sherif, M., Harvey, O.J., White, B.J. et al. (1961) *Intergroup Co-Operation and Competition: The Robbers Cave Experiment*. Norman: University of Oklahoma.

Shermer, M. (2017) Are we all racists? *Scientific American*, 317(2), 75.

Sheshkin, M. (2018) The inequality delusion. *New Scientist*, 237(3171), 28–31.

Shils, E.A. (1954) Authoritarianism: 'right' and 'left'. In R. Christie and M. Jahoda (eds.) *Studies in the Scope and Method of 'the Authoritarian Personality'*. Glencoe, IL: Free Press.

Sidanius, J. and Pratto, F. (1999) *Social Dominance: An Integrative Theory of Social Hierarchy and Oppression*. Cambridge, MA: Cambridge University Press.

Sidanius, J., Pratto, F. and Bobo, L. (1994) Social dominance orientation and the political psychology of gender: A case of invariance? *Journal of Personality & Social Psychology*, 67, 998–1011.

Sidanius, J., Pratto, F. and Bobo, L. (1996) Racism, conservation, affirmative action, and intellectual sophistication: A matter of principled conservatism or group dominance? *Journal of Personality & Social Psychology*, 70, 476–490.

Siegel, A.E. and Siegel, S. (1957) Reference groups, membership groups, and attitude change. *Journal of Abnormal & Social Psychology*, 55, 360–364.

Sinha, R.R. and Hassan, M.K. (1975) Some personality correlates of social prejudice. *Journal of Social & Economic Studies*, 3, 225–231.

Stainton-Rogers, R., Stenner, P., Gleeson, K. and Stainton-Rogers, W. (1995) *Social Psychology: A Critical Agenda*. Cambridge: Polity Press.

Starmans, C., Sheskin, M. and Bloom, P. (2017) Why people prefer unequal societies. *Nature Human Behaviour*, 1, 0082.

Stephan, W.G. (1978) School segregation: An evaluation of predictions made in Brown vs The Board of Education. *Psychological Bulletin*, 85, 217–238.

Stephan, W.G. and Stephan, C.W. (1985) Intergroup anxiety. *Journal of Social Issues*, 41, 157–175.

Stephan, W.G. and Stephan, C.W. (2000) An integrated threat theory of prejudice. In S. Oskamp (ed.) *Reducing Prejudice and Discrimination*. Mahwah, NJ: Lawrence Erlbaum Associates Inc.

Stern, W. (1912) *Die Psychologische Methoden der Intelligenzprufung*. Leipzig: Barth.

Stouffer, S.A., Suchman, E.A., LeVinney, L.C. et al. (1949) *The American Soldier: Adjustment During Army Life* (Vol. 1). Princeton, NJ: Princeton University Press.

Sue, D. and Sue, D.W. (1990) *Counselling the Culturally Different*. New York: John Wiley.

Sumner, W. (1906) *Folkways*. New York: Ginn.

Swann, W.B. (2011) Self-verification theory. In P. Van Lang, A. Kruglanski and E.T. Higgins (eds.) *Handbook of Theories of Social Psychology*. London: Sage.

Swann, W.B., Jr. (1983) Self-verification: Bringing social reality into harmony with the self. In J. Suls and A.G. Greenwald (eds.) *Social Psychological Perspectives on the Self* (Vol. 2). Hillsdale, NJ: Erlbaum.

Szasz, T.S. (1962) *The Myth of Mental Illness*. New York: Harper & Row.

Szasz, T.S. (1974) *Ideology and Insanity*. Harmondsworth: Penguin.

Tajfel, H. (1969) Social and cultural factors in perception. In G. Lindzey and E. Aronson (eds.) *Handbook of Social Psychology* (Vol. 3). Reading, MA: Addison-Wesley.

Tajfel, H. (1972) Experiments in a vacuum. In J. Israel and H. Tajfel (eds.) *The Context of Social Psychology: A Critical Assessment*. London: Academic Press.

Tajfel, H. (1978) *Differentiation Between Social Groups: Studies in the Social Psychology of Intergroup Relations*. London: Academic Press.

Tajfel, H., Billig, M.G., Bundy, R.P. and Flament, C. (1971) Social categorization and intergroup behaviour. *European Journal of Social Psychology*, 1, 149–178.

Tajfel, H. and Turner, J.C. (1979) An integrative theory of intergroup conflict. In G.W. Austin and S. Worchel (eds.) *The Social Psychology of Intergroup Relations*. Chicago, IL: Nelson-Hall.

Tajfel, H. and Turner, J.C. (1986) The social identity theory of intergroup behaviour. In S. Worchel and G.W. Austin (eds.) *Psychology of Intergroup Relations* (2nd edition). Monterey, CA: Brooks/Cole.

Talaska, C., Fiske, S.T. and Chaiken, S. (2003) *Biases Hot and Cold: Emotional Prejudices and Cognitive Stereotypes as Predictors of Discriminatory Behaviour*. Unpublished manuscript, Princeton University (cited in S.T. Fiske, 2004).

Tausch, N., Hewstone, M., Kenworthy, J.B. et al. (2010) Secondary transfer effects of intergroup contact: Alternative accounts and underlying processes. *Journal of Personality & Social Psychology*, 99, 282–302.

Taylor, S.E., Peplau, L.A. and Sears, D.O. (1994) *Social Psychology* (8th edition). Englewood Cliffs, NJ: Prentice-Hall.

Titus, H.E. (1968) Scale validity considered against peer nomination criteria. *Psychological Record*, 18, 395–403.

Triandis, H. (1990) Theoretical concepts that are applicable to the analysis of ethnocentrism. In R.W. Brislin (ed.) *Applied Cross-Cultural Psychology*. Newbury Park, CA: Sage.

Turner, J.C. (1985) Social categorization and the self-concept: A social-cognitive theory of group behaviour. In E.J. Lawler (ed.) *Advances in Group Processes: Theory and Research*. Greenwich, CT: JAI Press.

Turner, J.C., Hogg, M.A., Oakes, P.J. and Reicher, S.D. (1987) *Rediscovering the Social Group: A Self-Categorization Theory*. Oxford: Blackwell Publishing.

Turner, R.N. and Crisp, R.J. (2010) Imagining intergroup contact reduces implicit prejudice. *British Journal of Social Psychology*. https://doi.org/10.1348/014466609X419901

Turner, R.N., Crisp, R.J. and Lambert, E. (2007) Imagining intergroup contact can improve intergroup attitudes. *Group Processes & Intergroup Relations*, 10, 427–441.

Turner, R.N., Hewstone, M., Voci, A. et al. (2007) Reducing prejudice via direct and extended cross-group friendship. *European Review of Social Psychology*, 18, 212–225.

Tyerman, A. and Spencer, C. (1983) A critical test of the Sherif's Robbers Cave experiment: Intergroup competition and cooperation between groups of well-acquainted individuals. *Small Group Behaviour*, 14(4), 515–531.

Vaes, J., Leyens, J.P., Paladino, M.P. and Miranda, M.P. (2012) We are human, they are not: Driving forces behind outgroup dehumanization and the human-ization of the ingroup. *European Journal of Psychology*, 23, 64–106.

Vaes, J., Paladino, M. and Puvia, E. (2011) Are sexualized females complete human beings? Why males and females dehumanize sexually objectified women. *European Journal of Social Psychology*, 41, 774–785.

Vanneman, R. and Pettigrew, T.F. (1972) Race and relative deprivation in the urban United States. *Race*, 13, 951–957.

Vezzali, L., Capozza, D., Stathi, S. and Giovanni, D. (2012) Increasing outgroup trust, reducing infrahumanization, and enhancing future contact inten-tions via imagined intergroup contact. *Journal of Experimental Social Psychology*, 48, 437–440.

Vivian, J. and Brown, R. (1995) Prejudice and intergroup conflict. In M. Argyle and A.M. Colman (eds.) *Social Psychology*. London: Longman.

Vollhardt, J.R. (2009) The role of victim beliefs in the Israeli-Palestinian conflict: Risk or potential for peace? *Peace and Conflict: Journal of Peace Psychology*, 15, 135–159.

Wagstaff, G.F. and Quirk, M.A. (1983) Attitudes to sex roles, political conserva-tism and belief in a just world. *Psychological Reports*, 52, 813–14.

Walker, W.D., Rowe, R.C. and Quinsey, V.L. (1993) Authoritarianism and sexual aggression. *Journal of Personality & Social Psychology*, 65, 1036–1045.

West, K. and Hewstone, M. (2012) Culture and contact in the promotion and reduction of anti-gay prejudice: Evidence from Jamaica and Britain. *Journal of Homosexuality*, 59, 44–66.

Wetherell, M. (1982) Cross-cultural studies of minimal groups: Implications for the social identity theory of intergroup relations. In H. Tajfel (ed.) *Social Identity and Intergroup Relations*. Cambridge: Cambridge University Press.

Wetherell, M. (1996) Group conflict and the social psychology of racism. In M. Wetherell (ed.) *Identities, Groups and Social Issues*. London: Sage, in association with the Open University.

White, F.A. and Abu-Rayya, H.M. (2012) A dual identity-electronic contact (DIEC) experiment promoting short- and long-term intergroup harmony. *Journal of Experimental Social Psychology*, 48, 597–608.

White, F.A., Verrelli, S., Maunder, R.D. and Kervinen, A. (2018) Using electronic contact to reduce homonegative attitudes, emotions, and behavioural intentions among heterosexual women and men: A contemporary extension of the contact hypothesis. *Journal of Sex Research*, 1–13.

Wilson, G.D. (1973) *The Psychology of Conservatism*. New York: Academic Press.

Witt, L.A. (1989) Authoritarianism, knowledge of AIDS, and affect towards persons with AIDS: Implications for health education. *Journal of Applied Social Psychology*, 19, 599–607.

World Health Organization (2018–22) *International Classification of Diseases*. Geneva: WHO.